for Aaron —
wishing you tasty adventures
here in town. Come back
soon... so much to eat!
— geneva

UNIQUE EATS AND EATERIES

OF

SANTA BARBARA

GENEVA IVES

Copyright © 2017, Reedy Press, LLC
All rights reserved.
Reedy Press
PO Box 5131
St. Louis, MO 63139
www.reedypress.com

Library of Congress Control Number: 2017934680
ISBN: 9781681061092

All photos provided by the author unless otherwise noted.

Printed in the United States of America
17 18 19 20 21 5 4 3 2

DEDICATION

For my mother, who taught me to love surprises. My father, who
showed me how to go with the flow. And my husband, who treats
every meal like a celebration.

CONTENTS

INTRODUCTION

When people find out that you're a food writer, they inevitably get around to asking this question: "What's your favorite restaurant?"

I've been asked that more times than I can count, and I still don't have a good answer. I don't have one favorite restaurant; I have about two hundred. That means half or more of them couldn't even fit in this book. I have a favorite place to eat chilaquiles, a favorite diner to visit for soup when it's raining, and a favorite spot for ravioli. My favorites depend on how hungry I am, what time of the year it is, and the company I keep.

That's the fun part about eating in Santa Barbara. With hundreds of restaurants in a very small area, it's a "choose your own adventure" experience for hungry people. There are few national chains and plenty of local chef-driven and family-run businesses. Some places date back to the 1950s and others just opened last year. You'll find old bar cafes riddled with history down the street from new pop-ups serving fusion tacos.

In addition to restaurants, other kinds of food producers call this area home. If you're here long enough—or just happen to be in the right place at the right time—you're bound to meet fishermen, chocolatiers, farmers, and cheesemongers that supply many of the ingredients used in menus around town. Even if your appetite isn't inclined to try local sea urchin (although you really should) you'll find crowd-pleasing snacks including wonderful pickles, popcorn, and so much more in this little city by the sea.

The funny thing is, when I came to school here in the early 2000s (go Gauchos!), I don't remember the food landscape then being quite this varied. It's possible, even likely, that my budget was a factor. It's also possible that it just wasn't interesting yet. In chats with chefs and fellow food enthusiasts, it's been suggested that Santa Barbara restaurants have had to make rapid advances in the last decade to keep up with the gangbusters Central Coast wine scene. You can't pair fine wine with crummy food, after all. Well you can, but it's not exactly ideal.

But I think the most likely scenario is that the food was pretty good back then too; I just didn't know where to look. I hope this book will help some people with that.

My apologies in advance to the many great local restaurants that aren't listed in these pages. With fewer than one hundred opportunities, some fantastic dishes had to be left out. Maybe you weren't open when I submitted this, maybe no one has ever taken me to your place and shown me the secret joys of your menu, or maybe I just really, really want to keep you to myself. Please don't spit in my food when you see me next. If your eats are tasty, I promise I will find a way to make this glaring omission up to you.

I'd also like to apologize to my most patient, tireless, and long-suffering supporters. Waistband and wallet, I don't know where I'd be without you. Probably wandering pantsless and hungry somewhere.

And now with all of these silly sidebars and caveats out of the way, let's get to it! Some seriously delicious eats, right this way . . .

UNIQUE EATS AND EATERIES

OF

SANTA BARBARA

THE ANDERSEN'S DANISH BAKERY & RESTAURANT

If you're looking for pastry paradise, you've found it! This gilded Danish bakery is a downtown Santa Barbara institution for anyone with a sweet tooth. Opened in this location in 1978, the Andersen family has been serving up sugary concoctions for decades. Their motto is "do things right, or don't do them at all," and it shows in their attention to detail.

Although this charming sidewalk cafe also serves breakfast, lunch, and dinner, don't try walking out without at least one flakey morsel of dessert! In fact, the staff hands out samples right and left, so it's pretty much impossible to avoid.

People who prefer savory dishes will enjoy their omelets and quiches, but I think their more traditional Danish dishes are unique. Check out the open-faced smoked salmon sandwiches, pickled herring, and schnitzel.

Fun fact: this is one of the few places in town that offers high tea. Bring a friend or two and tuck into the tea of your choice paired with a tiered tower of petit fours, eclairs, and finger sandwiches.

The Andersen's also has full cakes available to take home for your special celebrations. Call ahead to get exactly the one you want.

1106 State St.
805-962-5085
andersenssantabarbara.com

Top right: The interior is every bit as sugary as the dessert menu. It's a fun stop for high tea.

Above left: The Andersen's sunny State Street patio is ideal for lunching and brunching.

Above right: This restaurant and bakery is best known for its sweet treats.

Type: Bakery, Sidewalk Cafe
Neighborhood: Downtown
Price: $$
Try the: French Waffle, Napoleon Hats, Marzipan
Great for: Dessert Dates, High Tea, Brunch

ARIGATO SUSHI

When you're looking for sushi in downtown Santa Barbara, Arigato is the place to go. The fish is fresh, the atmosphere is always lively, and the service is usually stellar. Open since 1985, this team knows what they're doing and has plenty of regulars to prove it. But there are two things you should know when you visit:

- They open at 5:30 p.m. every day.
- They do not take reservations.

The menu here is huge, which can be a good thing or a bad thing, depending on how you look at it. On the positive side, there are a lot of options. Even vegan and gluten-free diners will be able to order a satisfying meal. On the other hand, you have a lot of chances to order incorrectly and walk away wondering what all the fuss is about.

Okay, "incorrectly" might be a stretch. I can tell you what I order, but it might not work for your tastes. I prefer my sushi simple so I can taste the character of the fish. If you feel that way too, consider the salmon tartare, ahi carpaccio, and toro nigiri.

Would you rather have all the bells and whistles? Try the Pacific Rim Roll, a mouthful of a creation that includes yellowtail, asparagus, and chives topped with salmon, avocado, wasabi masago, yuzu tobiko with spicy aioli, wasabi vinaigrette, and chive oil. And don't miss the Mrs. Ebilyn—steamed pot stickers stuffed with shrimp and halibut.

Type: Japanese
Neighborhood: Downtown
Price: $$$
Try the: Nigiri, Urchin, Ankimo Hotate, Mrs. Ebilyn
Great for: Dates, People Watching, Bar Dining

Santa Barbara's most popular sushi restaurant, Arigato, opens at 5:30, and doesn't take reservations.

1225 State St.
805-965-6074
arigatosb.com

ARNOLDI'S CAFE

Take a trip to Italy without ever leaving Santa Barbara. Dine under the stars, sip wine, and play a little bocce ball on Arnoldi's sandy courts.

Established in 1937 by Giuseppe and Ilda Arnoldi, this restaurant brought the rich tastes of Northern Italy to town. In 1940, Giuseppe quarried local stone and built the restaurant that still stands at 600 Olive Street. Arnoldi's Cafe boasts a big, beautiful back patio with two bocce ball courts for recreational play . . . a great way to work out after eating some old-school gnocchi or lasagna.

Although the restaurant has changed hands over the years, its menu remains classic and largely unchanged. There are spicy marinaras, heavy alfredos, and milaneses fried just the way your mother used to cook them—if she was born in Lombardy like the Arnoldis were, anyway. The kitchen isn't open, but there is a window you can peek through to see the cooks hard at work stirring soups, rolling meatballs, and saucing pastas.

This might even be one of the few remaining holdouts to serve a classic antipasto plate. You should definitely give it a shot. Piled high with cold cuts, cheese-stuffed peppers, olives, and tomatoes, one order is enough to feed four. Getting a half-order and settling in at the beautiful old bar with a friend is a wonderful way to spend an hour.

That's right, the bar! While Arnoldi's does have a wine list, the full bar is inviting, and the drinks aren't too bad either. At least one Yelp reviewer complained that the mai tais here were "too rummy," which is 100 percent a compliment in my book. It's also kind of funny if

Type: Italian
Neighborhood: Downtown
Price: $$
Try the: Antipasto Plate, Lasagna Bolognese,
Milanese di Vitello
Great for: Families, Date Night, Special Events

Top right: Entrées like this gnocchi tricolore, sauced to represent the Italian flag, are filling.

Above left: Giuseppe Arnoldi quarried local stone for his restaurant in 1940. Photo by Aron Ives

Above right: Bocce after dinner is a local tradition at Arnoldi's. Photo by Aron Ives

you're a local, because Arnoldi's got its mai tai recipe from legendary Santa Barbara bartender Willy Gilbert, who was famous for his version of this tiki classic back at Jimmy's Oriental Gardens before it became The Pickle Room (where he still holds court).

Venturing outside, the patio is a delight, offering both sunlit seating and a plant-covered pergola area strung with lights. This is one of a handful of restaurants in Santa Barbara big enough to accommodate large (and loud) parties. If you sit outdoors, there's a good chance you'll be sharing space with a graduation, bachelorette, or birthday celebration.

On a balmy Santa Barbara night, there's nothing more timeless than heading to Arnoldi's with a few friends for drinks, dinner, and a little evening sporting.

600 Olive St.
805-962-5394
arnoldis.com

BACKYARD BOWLS

Backyard Bowls is a dietary staple for many locals. Although there are several locations—including a new foothold in Los Angeles—this entry is for the most charming of them all. Tucked in a small shopping center downtown between a coffee shop and a chocolate store, the ever-energetic team at Backyard Bowls is waiting to make all your healthy-eating dreams come true.

Its slogan says it all: Better life through better food. Serving acai bowls and nutritious smoothies, Backyard Bowls offers a healthy alternative for breakfast or lunch. Dig into a pile of bananas, strawberries, and goji berries stacked high atop a mountain of sweet, frozen acai berry pulp and housemade granola. Chilly and gray out? There are warm oatmeal, muesli, and quinoa bowls too. Most of the plant-based ingredients are organic, and none contain any chemicals or high-fructose corn syrup.

Type: Californian
Neighborhood: Downtown, Uptown, Goleta
Price: $
Try the: Backyard Bowl, Island Bowl, Pitaya Smoothie
Great for: Breakfast, Lunch, Post-Workout Refueling

Top left: Backyard Bowls has a sea of healthy options.

Above left: Try the Island Bowl: acai, banana, mango, pineapple juice, and coconut milk topped with bananas, strawberries, blueberries, coconut shavings, honey, and granola. Photo by Aron Ives

Above right: There are multiple locations in town now, but this one was the first.

Better still, Backyard Bowls engages in sustainable practices that are good for the planet. The restaurant is powered by wind energy, food scraps are composted, and to-go containers are biodegradable. Visit Backyard Bowls anytime you want to eat real food and feel really good about it.

331 Motor Way
805-845-5379
backyardbowls.com

BELLA VISTA

Chef Marco Fossati recently took the helm at Four Seasons Resort The Biltmore's restaurant, and already you can see a reinvigorated dining experience that combines Santa Barbara ingredients with techniques from his native Genoa, Italy. The updated menus are far from your standard hotel fare. Lunch is a mix of paninis, salads, and pizzas, for the most part, enlivened by ingredients that include housemade sausage, wild mushrooms, and bacon marmalade.

At dinner, dishes take a more indulgent turn. You might start with charcoal grilled calamari or traditional Tuscan ribollita soup. The shared charcuterie plate is the most popular appetizer on the menu, probably because Bella Vista is one of only twelve restaurants in California licensed to cure its own meats. Pasta is made onsite, so you'll definitely want to give it a shot. Then, for your main course, you may find yourself choosing between a thirty-day dry-aged New York steak or a whole branzino roasted with golden raisins and salsa verde.

While dinner is delicious, it might not be what the Bella Vista is most famous for. If you've ever talked to anyone in Santa Barbara about brunch—and price was no object—then you've undoubtedly heard of the "Biltmore brunch." Brunch at the Bella Vista restaurant is the stuff legends are made of: two whole rooms of food, bottomless mimosas, and hours to indulge while sitting on an ocean view patio. There is a seafood station, caviar station, cheese and charcuterie station, carving station, dessert station, and kid station (don't worry, it features tasty food for children, not actual kids) in addition to brunch specials and made-to-order egg dishes.

This grand buffet is open from 10 a.m. until 1:30 p.m. every Sunday. Brunch reservations are strongly recommended. A smaller, à la carte

Type: Italian
Neighborhood: Montecito
Price: $$-$$$
Try the: Brunch Buffet, High Tea, Branzino
Great for: Soirees, Romantic Evenings, Brunch

Top right: Dig into brunch with a side of sea breezes on Bella Vista's patio.

Above left: Chef Marco Fossati mixes local ingredients like uni with techniques from his native Genoa.

Above right: The flavorful menu changes with the seasons.

brunch is offered Monday through Saturday. On Saturday afternoons, the Bella Vista also hosts an afternoon tea with pastries and cakes and classic tea service. Reservations for tea are required twenty-four hours in advance.

Adjacent to the Bella Vista is the much more casual but still striking Ty Lounge. It may not be your everyday stop, but I think it's one of the most special places to grab a cocktail in Santa Barbara. It has a cozy fireplace in the winter, a sunny patio in summer, and one of the finest gin and tonic menus you've ever seen. Also on offer are tapas, pintxos, and heartier dishes, including an incredible local mussel special available Tuesdays and Wednesdays only.

Four Seasons Resort The Biltmore Santa Barbara
1260 Channel Dr.
805·969·2261
fourseasons.com/santabarbara/dining/restaurants/bella_vista

THE BLACK SHEEP

Like fancy food but hate stuffy atmospheres? The Black Sheep might be just the place for you. Located on a welcoming side street in downtown Santa Barbara, this is the kind of restaurant you hope to stumble into on your first night of vacation. The dining area is casual, with small tables, high ceilings, and a usually busy bar at one end.

Opened in 2014, a father-son team runs the show. Ruben Perez manages the restaurant and works the front of the house, while his chef father, Robert, leads the kitchen. "My dad and I have been working together since I was eight years old," said Ruben. "I was his unofficial waffle and pancake maker for a Sunday brunch for a restaurant he cooked at in Northern California. But we officially started working together around 1998."

The menu is a mix of global flavors and local ingredients. Think shoyu ramen, potato croquettes, and seriously delicious scallop crudo—after your first bite, you'll wonder why you ever even bother eating cooked scallops. Ingredients are organic, sustainable, and usually local. Nightly specials are always worth a try; you might have a foie gras taco or some wild boar stew.

More adventurous eaters will be happy to take a chance on the family-style tasting menu here. You'll sample multiple courses capped off with dessert for a good price, taking the stress out of what to order. Worried your whole party isn't quite ready to dig into a pâté of carrots roasted in duck fat? No problem. There's also a vegan/vegetarian chef's choice menu, so your veggie-loving friends and family members don't feel left out.

Type: New American
Neighborhood: Downtown
Price: $$–$$$
Try the: Scallop Crudo, Ramen, Chocolate Mousse
Great for: Dates, Bar Dining, Special Occasions

Top right: Father-and-son team Robert and Ruben Perez are responsible for The Black Sheep's culinary delights, like these wild boar ribs.

Above left: The menu changes frequently, but you'll always find hearty meats like this braised New Zealand lamb shank with Indian spice.

Above right: This restaurant shares a kitchen with Oveja Blanca, a fine dining seafood restaurant next door, and dishes frequently pass between them.

The Black Sheep doesn't serve cocktails in the traditional sense, but its beer and wine list is quite good. If you're into food and wine pairings, you'll be in good company here. Ruben is happy to talk you through your options. If you prefer to bring your own vintage, the corkage fee is reasonable.

"I love talking to our guests, and that they trust me to navigate their dining experience," he shared. "When tables are done eating and they give us hugs, handshakes, and high fives…that's why we do this!"

The Black Sheep shares a kitchen with Oveja Blanca, a fine dining seafood restaurant next door, so if you see something on that menu that you really want (and you're really nice about it when you ask), you just might get to experience the best of both worlds.

26 East Ortega St.
805 965-1113
theblacksheepsb.com

THE BLUE OWL

If scrambled eggs bore you and you think french toast is a total snooze, head to The Blue Owl for a meal guaranteed to wake up your taste buds. I put the restaurant type as "Asian Fusion" because I had to pick something, but really it should be "whatever Cindy Black feels like." The menu here is delicious, varied, and subject to change at any time, so don't get too attached to any one dish. The good news is that everything is tasty, so it's pretty hard to go wrong.

Like a lot of people in this seaside town of many colleges, Black came here for school—in her case, culinary school at Santa Barbara City College—and never left. She opened the first iteration of The Blue Owl in the fall of 2007. It was a late-night pop-up that operated out of another restaurant's kitchen in the middle of the downtown bar area on Thursday through Saturday nights, serving fried rice, burgers, and sandwiches wrapped in foil—the perfect food for fighting hangovers.

But The Blue Owl was so popular that people started going even when they weren't drinking…waiting until 10 p.m. on Thursday evenings just to get some grub. The wait started to get really long, and it was clear the business was outgrowing its shared space.

Fortunately for us hungry folks, in 2012 The Blue Owl got its own brick-and-mortar location and expanded hours to match. There's now a menu for lunch and dinner and a separate one for late night. The flavors are some of the most distinctive and exciting you'll find

Type: Asian Fusion
Neighborhood: Downtown
Price: $$
Try the: Crab Melt, Kim Cheezer, Thai Basil Burger
Great for: Lunch, Dinner, Late Night, Hipsters, Imbibers

Top right: The Kimcheezer—a grilled cheese packed with tangy kimchee—is a perennial favorite. Photo by Willhouse Photography

Above left: The Blue Owl serves lunch, dinner, and late night. Photo by Willhouse Photography

Above right: It's one of the few places to get bánh mì in Santa Barbara. Photo by Willhouse Photography

downtown, certainly at the price. Everything is well under $20 here. That includes dishes like their legendary Thai basil burger, crab melt, and pork bánh mì. "Most of my ingredients are organic, much of the produce is local, and a lot of work goes into it. We make our own kimchee for the grilled cheese, for example," said Black.

It's fun to come here in the late morning for brunch, hot coffee, and pie. It's equally enjoyable to stop in for lunch or dinner and a glass (or bottle) of wine or some draft beer. And late night is still kind of the entertaining madhouse it's always been.

One thing you should know if you do choose to eat here after dark—your order just may come with a side of sass. Black has been known to break out a microphone and heckle tipsy diners who don't pick up their food quickly enough, and the rest of the staff can be similarly snarky—for fun and kicks. You've been warned.

5 West Canon Perdido St.
805-705-0991
blueowlsb.com

BOATHOUSE

It might surprise you, but in Santa Barbara proper, there are only a few restaurants on the beach side of the street. The Boathouse is probably the best one, loved by locals and visitors alike. It's one of Santa Barbara's better seafood restaurants. Tucked away in a quiet part of town and facing Hendry's Beach, this is a great place to go for a romantic date, family dinner, or birthday celebration.

The space is gorgeous. There is a large patio that's sunny during the day and heated at night. A glass wall protects you from strong ocean breezes but allows for the most beautiful view in town. The dining room inside is lined with windows as well, allowing diners to gaze out at Arroyo Burro Beach, commonly referred to as Hendry's.

Enjoy fresh surf and turf and local Santa Barbara catches that often include spiny lobster and Dungeness crab. You can get light snacks, like ahi poke and steamed clams, as well as more decadent treats. This might be the only restaurant in town that serves chowder fries. Yep, that's a vat of golden french fries sprinkled with Old Bay, drenched in clam chowder, and topped with bacon. You should definitely try them.

Breakfast, lunch, and dinner are served daily. There's no better way to start your day than with a dolphin sighting while digging into a smoked salmon eggs Benedict.

The bar inside is two-sided with a window that opens out onto the patio where there are a few additional counter seats. The Boathouse's happy hour is generous and popular, usually extending from 3 p.m.

Type: Seafood
Neighborhood: Beachfront
Price: $$-$$$
Try the: Chowder Fries, Boathouse Signature Breakfast, Bloody Mary
Great for: Happy Hour, Brunch, Special Occasions

Top left: Fries topped with clam chowder? Yes, please!

Above left: The Boathouse is a popular spot for brunch. Try the huevos rancheros or smoked salmon eggs Benedict.

Above right: Dine on the patio for an uninterrupted view of Hendry's Beach.

until close Sunday through Thursday. Try the Boathouse Punch for a smooth tropical cocktail that tastes just like vacation. Refreshing blood orange margaritas are just $5, too!

The only drawback to visiting the Boathouse is that the parking is limited. Between the restaurant and the beach, it seems like the lot is always full. Try to carpool, visit in between normal meal times, or take a cab if you can. You can also park in the neighborhood across the street as a last resort (but I have a feeling the residents aren't too happy about that).

2981 Cliff Dr.
805-898-2628
boathousesb.com

BOUCHON

If you eat out frequently when you travel, you may be wondering if the Bouchon in Santa Barbara is affiliated with celebrity chef Thomas Keller's collection of Bouchon restaurants in Napa, Beverly Hills, and Las Vegas. It's not. But it is worth a visit (or two).

For cuisine that makes the most of regional ingredients, look no further than Bouchon. Vegetables are sourced from Santa Barbara's daily farmers' markets, and meat is purchased from local ranchers. Seasonal entrées include roasted venison medallions, braised Kurobuta pork shank, and crispy skin Pacific salmon. Two of its most popular dishes include the scallop trio and the maple-glazed duck breast.

On Tuesdays, you can take part in "Market Tour Tuesdays" if you reserve ahead. Join executive chef Greg Murphy at the Santa Barbara Certified Farmers Market for an informative foodie stroll and dinner. Guests rendezvous at the market, select items with the chef, and return for a three-course dinner with local wines for a set price.

Bouchon serves only dinner every night. Although menu items may seem meat-centric, Murphy gladly accommodates dietary needs and preferences. If you're vegetarian or vegan, your best bet is to leave your entrée up to him. He creates plates unique to the season that rival anything your more carnivorous companions may be eating.

Cheese plates and desserts are thoughtfully curated to pair with your meal. So is the wine list. Considerable in length and packed with local legends, it includes vintages available by the bottle and more than thirty served by the glass. Your server can help you

Type: Californian French
Neighborhood: Downtown
Price: $$$
Try the: Scallop Trio, Maple-Glazed Duck Breast, Rack of Lamb
Great for: Dates, Birthday Dinners, Private Parties

Top left: Chef Greg Murphy favors an "as fresh as possible" approach, featuring local catches like this pan-seared seabass. Photo by Shelly Vinson Photography

Above left: The freshly redone patio is open almost year-round. Photo by Shelly Vinson Photography

Above right: Bouchon is a great date-night destination. Photo by Shelly Vinson Photography

expertly pair wine with your order, but if, for some reason, you're not seeing what you want to drink, you can also ask for "The Outsider" list that includes champagnes and wines from other regions.

The interior dining space at Bouchon is cozy, with warm lighting and white tablecloths. A recently updated front patio allows for outdoor dining pretty much year-round. The Cork Room, a private dining room with an exclusive seasonal menu, is available for meetings and celebrations. Bouchon is intimate and romantic, the perfect place to take a date.

9 West Victoria St.
805-730-1160
bouchonsantabarbara.com

THE BREWHOUSE

Normally I don't lead with the fact that a restaurant has a menu just for dogs. But normally restaurants don't have dog menus, so I feel like in this case it's justified.

So before I tell you what humans get to eat here, let me tell you what's in store for Fido should you choose to bring him along. The "Brew-Dog Menu" includes chicken strips, burgers (plain), hot dogs, steak bites, vegetable patties, marrow bones, and biscuits and gravy. The problem with taking your four-legged friends to The Brewhouse is that they may never want to eat plain old kibble again.

For humans, the menu at this local brewpub is significantly larger. There's a full bar and a full menu of great comfort food. It's a fun place to visit for a pint and a bite with a group, your family, or a date. True to the business name, a variety of beers are brewed in house; some favorites include Apricot Wheat, Habanero Pilsner, and Baseball Saison. Once the beers are brewed and fermented onsite, they are transferred to serving tanks. The serving tanks then connect directly to the beer taps, assuring you the freshest pour.

The Brewhouse is a lively destination almost any time of day. Live bands play Wednesday through Saturday night every week, starting at 8:30 p.m. Happy hour happens every day—instead of being limited to school nights—and runs from 4 to 6 p.m. During these glorious two hours, you can get a lot of tasty snacks like french fries, oyster shooters, and jalapeño poppers for around $2. All beers are $1 off too.

Type: Brewpub
Neighborhood: West Beach
Price: $$
Try the: Beer, Gorgonzola Potato Chips,
Filet Mignon Enchiladas
Great for: Brunch, Groups, Dogs

Top left: The Brewhouse brews beer right here on the premises.

Top right: The drafts are always fresh, never having traveled more than a few feet from tank to tap.

Above left: A large menu makes The Brewhouse a great family stop for lunch or dinner.

Above right: You can even bring Fido—there's a full menu just for dogs!

An epic brunch bar appears on weekends and features optional bottomless mimosas. Children under twelve eat for free with one paid adult brunch meal, so it's a great excuse to drink in the daytime with your loved ones of all ages.

The Brewhouse is also the site of Santa Barbara's biggest Oktoberfest celebration each year. If you happen to be in town around that time of year and you like German food (and don't mind crowds), you don't want to miss this beer-laden celebration!

229 West Montecito St.
sbbrewhouse.com

BROPHY BROS.

No matter what I write about Brophy Bros., I'm sure I'm going to leave something important out. A Santa Barbara institution since it opened in 1985, this restaurant is part of the fabric of the town. Everyone has met a friend at the bar, had a bloody mary, and slurped a cup of clam chowder here.

Perched on top of a two-story building facing the Santa Barbara harbor, Brophy's serves up incredible scenery with a fresh seafood menu to match. The restaurant is anchored by a central bar that can be enjoyed both from inside and from the open-air patio.

There are raw oysters, steamed mussels, ceviche, and other small plates to start. Don't miss the garlic baked clams. Packed with breadcrumbs and topped with bacon, there's nothing else like them.

For larger appetites, there are salads, sandwiches, and fried plates. The fried shrimp and clam strips are especially good, as are the fish and chips. Daily specials don't really change daily, but they do feature fresh catches including swordfish, ahi, and other sea creatures.

Brophy's has won a lot of awards over the years. It's won dozens for best seafood restaurant and best clam chowder. It's also come up as a finalist for best bloody mary, which explains why you'll see patrons sipping the tomato-y cocktail at every hour of the day, including long after the sun has set.

All these mouthwatering eats paired with the tip-top location add up to one indisputable fact: Brophy's is never not busy. They also don't take reservations. It's strictly first come, first served here.

Type: Seafood
Neighborhood: Harbor
Price: $$
Try the: Bloody Mary, Garlic Baked Clams, Fish & Chips
Great for: Ocean Views, Impressing Visitors, Date Night

Top left: Try the fried calamari plate—a customer favorite that's tender, not tough.

Top right: The fresh sea air and harbor views really work up an appetite.

Above left: Oysters are always a good idea at Brophy Bros.

Above right: The cioppino is hearty and full of seafood. Do like the locals do and pair it with a bloody mary.

Go during unusual hours to avoid a long wait. Or go when you're not hungry . . . because you're certain to be famished by the time you're seated.

You have two other options if you're starving and trying to beat the wait. Although the upstairs restaurant usually has a line, you can visit the ground level bar for drinks and appetizers without checking in with the hostess. The view isn't as good, and the full menu isn't available. But you can get beer, clams, and cocktails, so that's pretty great. The family-operated group that owns Brophy Bros. also owns On The Alley, a more casual seafood pop-in around the corner with a few, but not many, of the same dishes. So that's another option, but I really think you should just stick it out and enjoy the view.

119 Harbor Way
805-966-4418
brophybros.com

CA'DARIO

Ca'Dario is a charming neighborhood Italian restaurant with an intimate setting, tucked just one block to the side of busy downtown State Street. Born and raised in Italy, owner Dario Furlati dishes up a menu featuring savory Northern Italian fare including pastas, daily risottos, rotisserie selections, a fresh fish of the day, succulent ossobuco, baked chicken, and grilled meats.

Furlati says his passion for food was born of spending time with his mother and grandmothers in their kitchens. He trained around Europe before setting up shop here in the American Riviera, where he has been a chef and partner in several local Italian restaurants. But this is his favorite and the one that bears his name.

It's also, my husband says, the place to go for the best steak in town. Another chef friend actually brought us here specifically for the steak on his birthday several years ago. To be exact, it's the Costata alla Fiorentina, a perfectly cut, twenty-four-ounce grilled rib eye steak, served with stewed white beans and sage. The steak is grilled and tender. And the soft white beans practically melt in your mouth, with surprise acidic bursts from the occasional piece of tomato.

Everything on the menu is tasty, but pay extra attention to the daily specials. Depending on the seasonal availability of certain ingredients, you might just catch something you're unlikely to find at another time of the year.

The wine list includes a wide range of Italian and Californian varietals. There is a full bar, if you prefer to start or finish your evening with a cocktail. The desserts are also quite good, if you happen to have

Type: Italian
Neighborhood: Downtown
Price: $$-$$$
Try the: Spaghettini con Fasolari, Costata alla Fiorentina, Ossobuco con Risotto
Great for: Dates, Special Occasions, Treating Yourself

Top: Visit Ca'Dario to try the Northern Italian fare of owner and chef Dario Furlati.

Above left: The small dining room fills up quickly every night.

Above right: Try sharing an order of Ravioli al Burro e Salvia to start. These housemade pasta pillows are filled with spinach and ricotta, then topped with brown butter and sage sauce.

saved some room. If not, lovely, sugary meringues come with your bill, so it's impossible to leave without a sweet aftertaste.

Since the restaurant is a local favorite, dinner reservations are recommended. Ca'Dario also has a very fun pizzeria two doors down. It's a more casual, pop-in place with a long bar, a TV usually tuned to sports, and an open kitchen with a view of the fiery hot pizza oven. If you feel like white linens and thoughtful service, go to Ca'Dario. But if you feel like a boisterous evening and maybe not using silverware? Ca'Dario Pizzeria might be just the ticket!

37 East Victoria St.
805-884-9419
cadario.net

C'EST CHEESE

At first, C'est Cheese was just a cheese shop. A rather glorious cheese shop, actually, filled to bursting with more than one hundred different kinds of cheese, as well as charcuterie, olives, and pretty much anything that makes a picnic fun. It smelled pungently beautiful, offered exotic cheese tastings, and was always happily busy.

So busy that it expanded.

While the adorable cheese shop is still the same place, C'est Cheese has taken over the two spaces next to it to offer a completely immersive cheese lifestyle experience. There is a bakery that churns out fresh pastries, tarts, and cakes, and a cafe with a full breakfast, lunch, and happy hour menu.

It's a wonderful place to visit for breakfast, whether you're in a hurry or have time to sit for a meal. The sun slants in nicely, the coffee is local, and there are delicacies like quiche, smoked salmon, and a breakfast grilled cheese on offer. Baked goods and coffee are available all day, but you have to go early if you're hoping to score a kouign-amann. Pronounced "queen ah-mahn," this ugly duckling cousin of the croissant tastes leaps and bounds better than it looks, simultaneously crunchy and soft, salty, and sweet with vanilla. It sells out in a flash!

At lunch, you can dig into grilled cheeses, assorted non-cheese sandwiches, soups, and salads. The cheese and charcuterie boards are a real treat. Perfect for sharing, each serves two to five people. These are best enjoyed sitting on the sunny patio, with a glass or bottle of wine from the shop.

Type: Cheesemonger/Cafe
Neighborhood: Downtown
Price: $$
Try the: Kouign-Amann, Breakfast Grilled Cheese
Great for: Weekday Lunch, Weekend Brunch, Happy Hour

Left: Settle into the cafe for a nice meal, and don't forget to pop into the adjacent cheese shop! Photo by Lindsay Baumsteiger

Right: Meet the kouign-amann, a heavenly pastry that sells out quickly. Photo by Lindsay Baumsteiger

In the late afternoon, C'est Cheese is a great stop for a pick-me-up before dinner. You can get assorted nibbles as well as beer and wine until 6 p.m. every day except Sunday. Just a few blocks off busy State Street, it's a nice hidden downtown destination after work.

If you love cheese but don't live in Santa Barbara—or you're a local who likes to have a steady supply of excellent cheese on hand—you might consider joining C'est Cheese's cheese club. It's like a wine club, except with more fragrant monthly shipments. A cheese and salami club membership is available too.

825 Santa Barbara St.
805-965-0318
cestcheese.com

CAJUN KITCHEN

This entry is for the Cajun Kitchen location in the center of downtown, but there is another one on De La Vina Street and still others in the neighboring towns of Goleta and Carpinteria, and they all have a similar menu. And probably a similar line on weekend mornings.

Owned by the Jimenez family since 1984, this breakfast and lunch destination is focused on diner classics with a Cajun twist. It's probably most popular for breakfast, when hungry families, students, and weekend vacationers converge. There are lots of different greasy-spoon-type items on the menu, so you're bound to see a few people hoping to recover from wicked hangovers as well. Heck, maybe you're one of them. I'm not judging—I've been there.

Hearty food, good prices, and quick service await you at Cajun Kitchen. Richard Jimenez Sr. was a prep cook when he took over, and the food feels like something genuine a cook would make to eat, rather than something conceived for a menu concept. Standard fare includes big, three-egg omelets, syrupy french toast, and classic sandwiches. Breakfast is served until 3 p.m. every day. In addition to the usual toast options, they also offer cornbread, biscuits, and blueberry muffins.

As the restaurant's name indicates, there are a number of Cajun dishes on the menu too. If your appetite leans savory in the morning, you might try the shrimp po'boy, blackened catfish, or gumbo. Or get your eggs served with jambalaya. I would say most people don't come for the Cajun food though, although the beignets are very tasty. If

Type: Diner/Cajun
Neighborhood: Downtown
Price: $
Try the: Beignets
Great for: Families, Hangovers, Breakfast All Day

Top right: Cajun Kitchen serves locally roasted Dune Coffee.

Above left: Hope you're hungry! The eggs Benedict on buttermilk biscuits is not for the faint of heart.

Above right: The menu is packed with both sweet and savory breakfast favorites.

you've eaten in New Orleans, it won't knock your socks off, but their scrambles and chilaquiles sure will.

One fun fact is that all Cajun Kitchens serve locally roasted Dune Coffee, made by the good folks at The French Press. So even though there is more than one location, it is still a very "Santa Barbara" place.

Because of the giant menu and casual atmosphere, this a great place to take kids, even if they're notoriously picky eaters. It's also a fun, informal place to dine with a group. Just prepare for a wait on weekends when the crowd comes running.

901 Chapala St.
805-965-1004
cajunkitchencafe.com

CHASE BAR & GRILL

I'm not going to tell you that the Chase has the best Italian food in town. It doesn't. I've been eating here somewhat regularly for the last ten years, and while the food is totally fine and sometimes even quite good, that's not why I go.

The Chase isn't a restaurant—it's a Santa Barbara tradition.

It has one of the best locations on State Street, and the atmosphere is dripping with romance. Thousands of twinkling white lights set the tone for a magical evening. Old standards by the likes of Frank Sinatra and Dean Martin float out from hidden speakers. It's a wonderful place to take a date or meet friends for a drink. The polished wood bar here has hosted thirsty patrons since the place opened in 1979.

If it's a weekend, holiday, or just plain nice evening out, be prepared to wait for a seat, especially on customary date nights. Your patience will be rewarded with great cocktails (especially if Todd is bartending) and a solid meal. Order any of the parmigianas or try the lasagna. Most entrées are served with soup or salad and pasta, definitely big enough to share. There is also a small patio set right on State Street, ideal for enjoying a glass of wine with someone special on a pleasant afternoon.

1012 State St.
805-965-4351
chasebarandgrill.com

Type: Italian
Neighborhood: Downtown
Price: $$
Try the: Lasagna, Eggplant Parmigiana, Martinis
Great for: Happy Hour, Date Night, Parade Viewing

Top: The menu here is classic Italian.

Right: The Chase is a fairy tale of twinkling lights and Sinatra classics.

CHINA PAVILION

Getting Chinese food at China Pavilion can be a pretty fun experience if you do it right. For starters, they have a tiny bar! It's often being used by the staff for folding napkins and other side work, but if you ask nicely, they will open it right up for you. It seats about four, has a TV, and serves up sweet tiki concoctions like zombies and mai tais in festive Polynesian glassware. You can even get a volcano—a giant rum drink that serves two.

After all of these cocktails, you will need some food, and their menu is solid with all the usual suspects. Try their crab Rangoon, kung pao anything, and the proprietary Silver Sprout Duck Soup. It's a little more expensive than you might be used to, but the restaurant is located in an impressively sized space in downtown Santa Barbara, and that can't be cheap. If you choose to eat in, you'll find it to be a little fancy too, with white tablecloths and comfortable chairs.

On the weekends, this is the only place in town with dim sum. It's usually full of folks sampling different dumplings, steamed buns, porridges, and egg custards. You should give it a try!

1202 Chapala St.
805-560-6028
china-pavilion.com

Left: The China Pavilion menu is made up of both familiar and specialty dishes. There's even a "secret" Chinese menu.

Right: This is the only place that serves dim sum.

Type: Chinese
Neighborhood: Downtown
Price: $$
Try the: Beef Pavilion Style, Fu Jian Fried Rice, Chicken Feet
Great for: Dim Sum, Tiki Drinks, Shared Meals

CHUCK'S OF HAWAII

If you look at reviews online, you'll find two very disparate views of Chuck's of Hawaii. The larger of the two factions loves Chuck's, although it's quite possible that these same reviewers have been regulars here since the 1970s. The smaller group doesn't understand Chuck's at all and will dock it points for dim lighting, throwback décor, and an unchanging menu.

While everything the latter party complains about is true, don't let it stop you from going to Chuck's and having a marvelous time. This is a steakhouse where the ceilings are low, the lighting is dark, the interior is decidedly dated, and the mai tais flow like water. It's the kind of place you go with your favorite people for a dinner full of inside jokes, rum, and red meat. If you prefer brightly lit, sparsely decorated interiors and beautifully plated dishes that photograph well for social media, this isn't your restaurant.

Since 1967, lit tiki torches have guided hungry patrons into the parking lot of Chuck's. Open only for happy hour and dinner, the restaurant offers hand-cut steaks, grilled vegetables, and an array of fresh local and imported seafood. Saunter through a sea of Hawaiian shirts and hatch-cover tables—a nod to founder Larry Stone's travels through the South Pacific—to explore Chuck's award-winning salad bar, stocked with everything that makes lettuce a joy to eat, including rich dressings, sesame cauliflower, and housemade croutons.

Food isn't the only draw here. At the front of the restaurant, Chuck's bar is long and comfortable. Locals will attest that it's the perfect place to settle in for a cocktail or two. Happy hour

Type: Steakhouse
Neighborhood: Upper State
Price: $$-$$$
Try the: Mai Tai, Salad Bar, Teriyaki Rib Eye
Great for: Family Dinners, Date Nights, Bar Dining

Top left: Hankering for a hunk of steak? Chuck's has been a Santa Barbara tradition since 1967.

Above left: When you see flaming tiki torches, you know you're at the right place.

Above right: Don't pass go without getting a mai tai at this Hawaiian-themed restaurant.

means popping in for a refreshing adult beverage paired with a complimentary appetizer plate comprising cheddar cheese, crackers, and pepperoncini.

Is heart-healthy grape juice more to your liking? Chuck's also has a wide selection of wine available. Its list combines the local and not-so-local seamlessly. It has even won *Wine Spectator*'s Award of Excellence for the last twenty-eight years and counting.

Every January, Chuck's celebrates its anniversary and rolls prices back on select items for an entire week. While the menu is more limited, this annual event always draws a crowd. If you're planning to visit during this time, be sure to get a reservation!

3888 State St.
805-687-4417
chucksofhawaii.com

COLD SPRING TAVERN

Sometimes you just want to chill out and have a meal at a place where other people also ate a meal way back in, say, 1865. Sound familiar? When that mood strikes, Santa Barbara has just the restaurant for you.

If you're in the area (or even passing through), it would be a complete and utter shame—and possibly a lifelong regret—to miss Cold Spring Tavern. Established along a stagecoach route, this bar and restaurant has been serving road-weary travelers since the late nineteenth century. Travel back in time to enjoy lunch or dinner in this wooden, cabin-style eatery set back in the Los Padres National Forest.

The menu here dishes up hearty burgers, steaks, and even game like rabbit and venison. The interior is dark and cozy. Taxidermy, vintage photos, and four fireplaces decorate the dining rooms. Breakfast is served on the weekends. You can get a wild game omelet, grilled pork chop, or country fried steak, among other things.

The real draw at Cold Springs, though, is the tri-tip. Served only on the weekends and not in the dining room, the tri-tip sandwich is well worth the twenty-minute-or-so drive from downtown. Hang out outside, listen to the live music, and dig into a fluffy bun full of warm meat cooked over an open fire.

Here are a couple of pointers to help you have the best possible time:

- Load up at the au jus station. Pour a little on your sammy and then take a few extra cups for dipping.
- Try the other sauces. The hot mustard is quite nice, but locals tend to prefer the salsa.

Type: American
Neighborhood: Los Padres
Price: $$
Try the: Tri-Tip, Chili, Venison
Great for: Weekends, Families, Dates

Top left: Opened in 1865, Cold Spring Tavern has been an area watering hole for more than a century. Photo by Aron Ives

Above left: The restaurant serves a full menu of hearty game favorites, but on the weekends everyone comes up for the tri-tip sandwich.

Above right: The tavern is home to live music every week.

- Want your meat rarer or more well done? Be nice at the counter. A tip never hurts.
- Go early. It's not uncommon for the tri-tip to sell out before 3 p.m. Also, parking can be tricky when it's busy.

Cold Springs Tavern draws a varied and friendly crowd. Families, couples on dates, groups of people on their way to or back from wine tasting in Los Olivos—all are welcome here. And on any given day, you're likely to see the flash of chrome as you pull up. If you have a bike, you'll be in good company.

One more quick thing I just want to add about this place— although he's from Oklahoma, my incredible father-in-law, Michael Ives, used to hang out here when he went to college in Santa Barbara back in the 1970s. If you've met him, you know he's one hell of a man, and that's recommendation enough.

5995 Stagecoach Rd.
805-967-0066
coldspringtavern.com

CORAZÓN COCINA

Operated by chef Ramón Velazquez and his charming, endlessly enthusiastic staff, Corazón Cocina offers up a fresh, affordable Mexican spread worthy of royalty.

Prepare to experience love at first sight when you lock eyes with Velazquez's pork belly quesadilla, bursting with onions, cheese, and homemade salsa. And his ceviche tostadas—some dressed with coconut milk and topped with pomegranate seeds—will have you drooling.

The menu at Corazón Cocina changes depending on what is in season. "Market" dishes, like market tacos or market quesadillas, are frequently offered to showcase ingredients that are currently available at the Santa Barbara Certified Farmers Market. A recent visit yielded a tempura cauliflower taco cooked with local dates.

To drink, enjoy housemade aguas frescas or almond milk horchata. Beer, iced tea, and soda are also available. Place your order at the counter, then stock up on freshly made salsas while you wait. Seating is first come, first served, but if it's full, there are plenty of places around the market to sit. There's a sunny patio outside too.

Type: Mexican
Neighborhood: Downtown
Price: $-$$
Try the: Ensenada Taco, Sayulita Tostada,
La Gringa Quesadilla
Great for: Casual Dates, Quick Lunches, Take Out

Top left: The Ensenada taco at Corazón Cocina is the most flavorful fish taco in town.

Above left: Ceviches here are always fresh and change to reflect seasonal ingredients. Photo by Julia Garcia

Above right: Specials change daily but are always colorful. Photo by Julia Garcia

Corazón Cocina is open for lunch and dinner every day of the week. Popular items frequently sell out early in the afternoon, so plan ahead if you want access to everything on the menu.

38 West Victoria St.
805-845-0282

D'ANGELO BREAD

For a bistro-style breakfast or lunch treat, pop into D'Angelo Bread. This combination bakery and restaurant is situated just off State Street in the historic part of downtown Santa Barbara. From perfectly poached eggs and personal-sized Bundt cakes to finger sandwiches served with local greens, D'Angelo has something for every appetite.

The interior is cozy, with a row of small tables along the front of the bakery. The outdoor patio is dog friendly and ideal for getting a little sun while socializing with fellow diners and passersby.

Settle in and order a meal that highlights freshly made bread. The Eggs "Rose" is justifiably famous around these parts—two poached eggs served atop savory olive bread smeared with lemony artichoke spread. Pair it with a latte or a pot of loose-leaf tea to start your day on the right foot.

D'Angelo does not take reservations. Seating is strictly first come, first served, and there can be a significant wait on the weekends. In a hurry? Table service can be slow at peak hours, but you can always walk up to the counter for fresh coffee, warm baked goods, and housemade loaves of bread to go. The baguettes and pastries are delicious and perfectly wonderful for snacking on at home or on the go.

25 West Gutierrez St.
805-962-5466
dangelobread.com

Left: The Eggs "Rose" are justifiably famous here. Two eggs poached to order atop kalamata olive bread smeared with a lemony artichoke spread.

Right: In a hurry? Take incredible bread to go.

Type: Bakery
Neighborhood: Downtown
Price: $$
Try the: Olive Bread, Eggs "Rose," Huevos Rancheros
Great for: Coffee, Breakfast Meetings, Brunch

DAVE'S DOGS

Dave Reynoso, the man who makes hot dogs that I literally dream about, started out in an office job like anyone else. Then one day a retiring coworker pulled him into an office, shut the door, and said, "You are too young to be stuck here for thirty years like I was. Go out and pursue your dreams."

And so the best hot dog cart in town was born. Stop by any night except Sunday, usually from around 6 p.m. until midnight, to try incredible hot dog creations for less than $10. There are dogs topped with avocado and cilantro, and others with pepperoni or mac 'n' cheese. And you can add bacon to all of them!

"I set out to be the guy to take hot dogs to a new level of uniqueness in Santa Barbara," said Reynoso. "I am making my dream hot dogs and sharing them with everyone who comes out to support Dave's Dogs."

Turkey dogs are also available. Even more exciting (at least for a certain subset of diners who often feel left out of "fast food" options), veggie dogs are an option too. More toppings, more value, more dogs . . . what are you waiting for?

134 South Milpas St.
805-895-2802

Type: Hot dogs
Neighborhood: Eastside
Price: $
Try the: Santa Barbara Dog, Weekly Special
Great for: Friend Meetups, Vegetarians, Late Night

Top left: Owner Dave Reynoso is living his dream of creating fully loaded hot dogs for very happy customers.

Top right: Dave has something for everyone, including these veggie dog creations.

Left: Feeling spicy? Try the Jalapeño Popper Dog.

DOWNEY'S

For an intimate restaurant with incredible food and service, take a trip to Downey's. It's a little fancy looking from the outside—all white linens and muted tones—but don't let that intimidate you. Stop to read the frequently updated menu out front, and you'll want to make a reservation at once.

Downey's is consistently rated as one of the best restaurants in Santa Barbara in terms of crowdsourced data, from Yelp to Zagat. Chef John Downey and his wife Liz have expertly delighted guests in this downtown location for decades, dishing up some of the finest farm-to-table foods before such a restaurant concept even had a name.

The dining room may be a little more formal than you're used to (hint: you really should dress up), and so is the service. And that particular detail feels refreshing in a laid-back beach town where servers tend to be a little more casual.

I can't say it better than the website does: "If you would like to enjoy a true Santa Barbara dining experience where you will not be rushed, but cared for, we invite you to visit Downey's for dinner." You will never find yourself trying to get your waiter's attention, out of water, or otherwise inconvenienced while you're eating here.

All that said, Downey's focus steadfastly remains on food made with the highest-quality ingredients—not trends, not décor, not celebrity. As a result, John's dishes are finely created and executed, as evidenced by ragout of local lobster with chanterelles, Carpenter

Type: California-French
Neighborhood: Downtown
Price: $$$
Try the: Market Soup, Lobster Salad, Grilled Duck
Great for: Date Night, Quiet Special Occasions, High Falutin'

Top left: Owner and chef John Downey creates mouthwatering dishes at the restaurant he operates with his wife, Liz.

Top right: Or try something a little more indulgent like this raspberry white chocolate cream pie.

Above left: Finish your meal with freshly made ice cream.

Above right: Entrées rotate frequently, but you might find this natural Angus filet mignon with balsamic sauce, grilled asparagus, and roast potato if you're lucky.

Ranch squab with braised mustard greens, and grilled duck with cabernet sauce. Steak, lamb, and fresh fish also figure into the ever-changing menu.

Liz Downey manages the front of the house and is often present in the dining room to answer questions and help you select California wines that pair with your meal. Her thoughtfully done plein air paintings hang on the walls too. Because really, Downey's is more than a restaurant. It's a heartwarming love story, and the main characters are John and Liz, food, and Santa Barbara.

1305 State St.
805-966-5006
downeyssb.com

DUTCH GARDEN

"Where State turns into Hollister and dreams come true." That is the unofficial slogan my husband has given to this hidden German restaurant. Even a lot of locals don't know about it. Or maybe they do, but they haven't been in because it looks like just some old diner with a windmill on the sign.

It is old, that's true. In fact, the Dutch Garden was opened in 1949, making it one of the three oldest continuously operating restaurants in town. The food is most decidedly German, not Dutch, but if it had been named "German Garden" after World War II, it might not have fared so well. And that would be sad for those of us who love sauerkraut, potato pancakes, and schnitzel dishes.

There are three seating options when you arrive. You can choose to sit inside at the ten-seater bar counter or in the dining room that's filled with taxidermy, beer steins, gnomes, and faux ivy. Or, when the weather's nice, you can sit outside in the beer garden, surrounded by trees.

Husband and wife Ken and Laurie Luetjen have been at the helm here for more than thirty years. Ken does most of the cooking in a small kitchen you can watch from the counter. The happily constant menu boasts hearty portions of various meats, paired with sides of potato pancakes, red cabbage, and other vegetable dishes. It may not be a vegetarian's dream destination, but you can order a plate of just side dishes and leave quite full. There's also a fish special every night.

Type: German
Neighborhood: Upper State
Price: $$
Try the: Duck, Eisbein Special, Soup
Great for: Bar Dining, Beer Gardens, Lunch, Dinner

46

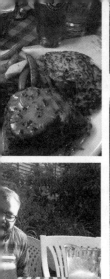

Top left: Dinners are anything but light. Expect a plate piled with meat, veggies, sauerkraut or red cabbage, and potato pancakes or German potato salad.

Above left: Outside there's more beer and also sunshine.

Above right: You might be tempted to drive right past this little roadside restaurant, but you shouldn't!

Every meal comes with soup or salad. Be smart and order the soup. Ken is famous—at least locally—for his soup. He makes everything from borscht and carrot almond to sorrel and chicken noodle.

The Dutch Garden has a great selection of German and Belgian beers available by the bottle or on draft. Even if you're not hungry, the beer garden can be a great place to share a pitcher of lager on a sunny day.

Be aware that a very small team runs this restaurant. In addition to Ken and Laurie, there may be either one or two waiters on shift. It is not the place to go if you are in a rush. Likewise, when they are done for the day, they are done. The Dutch Garden is open Wednesday through Saturday from 11 a.m. to 8 p.m. The considerate thing to do is to arrive by 7 p.m. at the latest.

4203 State St.
805-967-4911

EAST BEACH TACOS

You might think it's a little strange that this book is sending you to the batting cages to eat, but bear with me. I'm about as sporting as a sloth, but the second someone suggests a trip to this place, I lace up my shoes like a pro athlete. Well, that's a lie. I do slip on my sandals *really* quickly though.

East Beach Tacos is a small taco shack serving up one of the most inventive taco menus, with a view of aspiring baseballers. You can get fresh tuna poke tacos served in wonton shells, bánh mì-inspired tacos, and crispy fried fish and shrimp creations.

And the menu isn't just limited to tacos. They have a number of other yummy snacks, including the Beach Ball—a seasoned rice ball filled with spicy tuna and sprinkled with sea salt and sesame seeds.

The one caveat is that parking is extremely limited, and the lot is tight to turn around in when it's full. If you plan on having any of the delicious, affordably priced beer and wine they serve here, you might be better off finding a spot on the street. Or, you know, pulling a Geneva and getting your friend to drive.

226 South Milpas St.
805-770-2761
eastbeachtacos.com

Type: Seafood
Neighborhood: East Beach
Price: $
Try the: Poke Tacos, Gangnam Tacos, Beach Ball
Great for: Lunch, Cheap Dates, Groups

48

Top left: Try the Beach Ball, a seasoned rice ball filled with spicy ahi tuna, scallions, and sesame seeds.

Above left: The Triple Play is the best deal on the menu, letting you try three tacos for less than $10.

Above right: This tiny restaurant tucked by the batting cages is a taco lover's dream.

EMPTY BOWL GOURMET NOODLE BAR

This is the place to grub down if you're craving something fresh, salty, spicy, and sweet. Empty Bowl Noodle Bar is located inside the Santa Barbara Public Market, an open-plan shopping center that is a must-visit for hungry people and foodies. This indoor market contains a collection of specialty merchants and restaurants, including Empty Bowl.

With a menu that will make your mouth water, Empty Bowl serves regional noodle bowls and specialty small plate appetizers from Thailand and Taiwan. Start with a colorful green papaya salad before you move on to something more substantial. The soups are meat based, but many of the noodle plates have vegetarian options (just be sure you ask them to cook without fish sauce). Every dish is made fresh to order in their open kitchen. You can watch the team cook your food while you wait.

And wait you will. Empty Bowl does not take reservations—no matter who you are or pretend to be. The bar fits, well, about sixteen by my count, and those seats fill up fast. If you're dining with a large party, this might not be the place for you. But it's a wonderful dining option for travelers who are eating alone.

Empty Bowl does a nice job of balancing bright flavors in every dish. But thrill seekers will like the neat lineup of peppers on the dining counter that lets you add your preferred amount of heat. If

Type: Thai
Neighborhood: Downtown
Price: $$
Try the: Green Papaya Salad, Pancit Noodles,
Northern Thai Curry Noodle
Great for: Lunch, Solo Diners, Spice Enthusiasts

Top left: Mama's dumplings are filled with ground pork shoulder, napa cabbage, and minced fresh ginger.

Above left: Bangkok street noodles are a soupy mixture of thin rice noodles, BBQ pork, minced pork, pork meatballs, fish sauce, bean sprouts, Chinese broccoli, fried wonton skin, green onions, cilantro, fried garlic, crushed peanuts, and dried chiles.

Above right: The Northern Thailand curry noodle "Khoa Soi" soup is filling and sells out frequently.

you're a little too enthusiastic with the spice, cool things down with a refreshing beverage. In addition to heavenly Thai iced teas, Empty Bowl has an impressive beer and wine lineup. Try a local IPA on draft or get a bottle of rosé to pair with your summer rolls.

If you're too impatient to jostle for a seat at this popular restaurant, you do have two other options. You can either take your food to go or take your food "kind of to go" and stay inside the market for an urban picnic. There are plenty of communal tables you can snag, plus there's the added benefit of being able to bring over food from other vendors. Or you can transport your order down to the wine bar at the back of the market and enjoy an afternoon tipple or two.

38 West Victoria St. #109
805-335-2426
emptybowlnoodle.com

FARMER BOY RESTAURANT

Farmer Boy has been a local dining institution since 1958. This diner-style eatery in the upper State area is a great place to grab a bite outside the hustle and bustle of downtown. It serves breakfast and lunch comfort foods made to order with fresh ingredients.

A recent renovation revived the property, menu, and patrons. The family behind the eternally popular Brophy Bros. seafood restaurant at the harbor took it over and reopened it in 2015. And while some things are brand-spanking new—thank goodness—many classic menu items are still available, including their ooey-gooey cinnamon rolls.

For breakfast, try an egg scramble or some chicken and waffles. The biscuits are also extremely popular. At lunch, grab a hearty beef or salmon burger or try the fish and chips. Prices here are quite reasonable. Most dishes ring up under $15, even the crab cakes!

The inside has cozy booths as well as a long dining counter that can host casual parties or single patrons. There are also a few small tables outside. One of the most striking design elements is the Andy Warhol-esque wall of ketchup at the back of the restaurant. It's practical and pretty, a lot like the rest of the diner.

3427 State St.
805-845-6749
farmerboy.com

Type: Diner
Neighborhood: Upper State
Price: $$
Try the: Fried Chicken & Waffles,
Cinnamon Roll
Great for: Breakfast, Brunch, Family Meals

Top left: Classic diner neon flashes above the long dining counter.

Above left: Farmer Boy pancakes are served with whipped butter and warm maple syrup.

Above right: The chicken and waffles will set you up for a great day ahead. You can even add extra chicken for a very reasonable cost.

FLAVOR OF INDIA

Exotic cuisine in Santa Barbara tends to fall into three main categories: Mexican, Italian, and sushi. Some noodle shops have added welcome flavor to the area in the last decade or so. But I'm most thankful for places that have been around for years even though they fall outside of the Santa Barbara trifecta.

Flavor of India is such a place.

This family-owned Indian restaurant has been serving lunch and dinner on upper State Street for more than twenty-five years. It's one of the first places I ate when I moved to town for college. Flavor of India has won dozens of local awards for best Indian food.

They serve traditional Indian items including samosas, kormas, and tandoori dishes. Their onion bhaji is crisp and delicious. If you like chai tea, you should definitely try theirs. It's spicy and rich, and you get endless refills.

They serve lunch and dinner Monday through Saturday. A lunch buffet is available in addition to the full menu. Beer and wine are also served. Takeout is an option as well. Free parking is available behind the restaurant or on the street out front.

3026 State St.
805-682-6561
flavorofindiasb.com

This Indian restaurant on upper State Street has won dozens of readers' choice awards.

Type: Indian
Neighborhood: Upper State
Price: $$
Try the: Chai
Great for: Weekday Lunches, Family Dinners

THE FRENCH PRESS

Okay, okay, so The French Press is a coffee shop (actually it's a really good coffee shop with three locations), but I promise you that it's worth a visit if you're hungry.

Here's why: all their pastries are made in house. At this very location. And they're super scrumptious. We're not talking about dry blueberry scones and stale coffee cake. Instead, plan on being faced with some tough decisions when you peer into the pastry case. Do I want a seasonal fruit galette? A savory scone? A warm biscuit with fresh jam?

"The bakery shares the kitchen with the cafe and is on the other side of a wall from where we roast all of our coffee. This has meant that we can be really collaborative and pair our coffees with seasonal snacks," said Julia Mayer, who opened the first location with her husband in 2009. "That we are across the street from the weekly farmers' market hasn't hurt either! There is so much seasonal deliciousness grown here in Santa Barbara. We have really taken advantage of the opportunity to use the bakery to showcase the local produce."

Of course, you'd be remiss to leave without a latte or, better still, a bag of beans. Like Mayer mentioned, an incredible selection of single-origin coffees is roasted right onsite.

528 Anacapa St.
805-962-7733
dunecoffeeroasters.com

Above left: The French Press's toast program offers homemade breads spread with both sweet and savory toppings.

Above right: This local coffee shop not only roasts its own beans but also makes all its own pastries.

Type: Bakery/Coffee Shop
Neighborhood: Downtown
Price: $
Try the: Biscuits, Toast, Galettes
Great for: Coffee Dates, Study Breaks, Freelancers

GARRETT'S OLD FASHIONED RESTAURANT

When Guy Fieri came to town to test out Santa Barbara diners, drive-ins, and dives for his television show, he didn't stop here, and I have no idea why. Garrett's Old Fashioned Restaurant is a diner of the highest order. There's a long bar with stools that only kind of swivel, booths with longhorn emblems in the table tops, coffee pots that never run out, and a friendly staff that knows their regulars.

Open every day for breakfast and lunch, Garrett's serves up classic greasy spoon menu items with a smile. People love the omelets and hash browns, as well as the Monte Cristo sandwiches packed with ham and cheese and dusted with powdered sugar. At lunch the patty melt is popular, but you can get it in the morning too if you feel like starting your day with something beefy.

The secret to a perfect order here is this: no matter what you decide to eat, you should also order at least one fresh blueberry pancake. Sometimes there are two kinds of blueberry pancakes, one with fresh blueberries and one with jarred blueberries, so be sure to specify. I promise you—as someone who doesn't even particularly care for pancakes—that it's like taking a warm, fluffy, juicy bite of heaven!

2001 State St.
805-569-0400

Left: Prices are reasonable, service is great, and there are longhorns embossed on the tables.

Right: Garrett's is a great greasy spoon located in the original McConnell's ice cream shop building.

Type: Diner
Neighborhood: Downtown
Price: $
Try the: Blueberry Pancakes, Omelets,
Monte Cristo Sandwich
Great for: Early Breakfast, Late Breakfast,
Families, Hangovers

THE HABIT BURGER GRILL

Before The Habit became one of the great American burger chains, it was a single little shack near the beach. This location is the original one, opened in 1969 by two brothers who wanted to serve a great burger at a great price. Almost five decades later, that still holds true.

Renowned for its charburgers, the restaurant uses a stainless steel charbroiler with a cast-iron grill to sear smoky flavors into every patty placed on its fiery grates. But beef isn't your only choice here. There are also chicken, veggie, and line-caught tuna sandwiches and salad options, making it an ideal casual destination for any group. You can have your burger served on grilled sourdough (highly recommended) and pair it with fries, sweet potato fries, onion rings, or tempura green beans. And more importantly, this Habit is the only one that serves chili fries and burgers.

This location has covered outdoor seating. It's a nice place to sit down and watch the world drive by, but if you're in a hurry—or it's packed—you can also take your food to go.

Worth knowing: they have a truck that you can rent to cater weddings, parties, and corporate events. It's a surefire way to become the best boss, in-law, or other authoritative figure in town!

5735 Hollister Ave., Goleta
805-964-0366
habitburger.com

Left: You've probably heard of The Habit, but did you know this is the original location?

Right: It's a fast, convenient stop for burgers, veggie burgers, and freshly made shakes and malts.

Type: Burgers
Neighborhood: Goleta
Price: $
Try the: Santa Barbara-Style Char, Chili Fries, Chocolate Malt
Great for: Family Meals, Casual Dining, Takeout

HARRY'S PLAZA CAFE

Do you like stiff drinks and hearty portions? You do?! Then you better hightail it on down to Harry's Plaza Cafe, a local favorite for almost half a century. Chicagoan Harry Davis opened this place in 1968, and it has all the bells and whistles of a classic steakhouse. Cherry red vinyl booths? Check. Mirrored bar? Yep. Stony-faced animal taxidermy? You know it!

Settle into your seat and order a cocktail before you take in the sights. If you're a fan of martinis, you're in luck. At Harry's they serve them with a little extra in the shaker, so you can refill your drink without having to wait.

Now that you're not so parched, it's time to have a more serious look around. The history of Santa Barbara is proudly displayed in more than fifteen hundred photographs that cover the walls. There are aerial photos of downtown before it was paved, snapshots of local characters, and autographed celebrity portraits. And the moose head in the front room? Legend has it that it was actually a pet, owned by one of Harry's friends and customers. When the moose died of natural causes, his head was preserved and presented to Harry as a gift.

Don't expect to find any wild game (or pets) on the menu though. The menu at Harry's dishes up classic American comfort food. Think shrimp cocktails, chopped salads, beef dip sandwiches, steaks, and seafood. You can even get breakfast all day if that's the sort of thing you like. The kitchen is located right by the front door, partially glassed off so you can watch the cooks work.

Type: American
Neighborhood: Upper State
Price: $$
Try the: Harry's Hurricane, Jalapeño Bottlecaps, Burnt Ends Sandwich
Great for: Double Dates, Family Dinners, Celebrations

Top left: Decades of Santa Barbara history hang on the walls above Harry's beloved red booths.

Above left: The menu is packed with comfort food favorites.

Above right: Have a special event coming up? Reserve the Ranchero Room for your party . . . it even has its own bar.

Although Harry is sadly no longer with us, a large painting of him in his Harry's uniform, hard at work polishing glasses, hangs between the kitchen and the bar, forever keeping an eye on things.

For a piece of living history, ask if Renee is working. This veteran server has waited tables at Harry's for more than thirty-five years. She's such an icon that people—both men and women—dress up as her for Halloween around these parts. Don't believe it? Just scan the walls. You'll soon find the photos to prove it.

3313 State St.
805-687-2800
harryssb.com

THE HITCHING POST II

Yes, this is the restaurant you saw in that movie with the two guys who drank a lot of wine. While The Hitching Post II may have achieved international fame when it was featured in the 2004 film *Sideways*, it has always been a favorite of Santa Barbara locals.

Although not technically in Santa Barbara city, it's still in the county and definitely worth the half-hour drive. The nightly dinner menu combines traditional Santa Maria-style barbecue with local ingredients and contemporary cooking techniques for a steakhouse feel that's full of flavor.

Santa Maria style dictates that the meat is seasoned and then cooked over native red oak on a cast-iron grill over the coals. The main attraction at The Hitching Post II is their indoor barbecue, staged behind glass, where guests can watch the chefs grill massive quantities of steaks and chops over a live wood fire.

The Hitching Post II is a family business. Owner, chef, and winemaker Frank Ostini actually started helping out in the kitchen at his father's restaurant—The Hitching Post in Casmalia, California—way back in 1976. A short stint turned into a prolonged stay as the Ostinis opened this, their second restaurant, in 1986. In 1993, Ostini took over as sole proprietor of this restaurant location.

Ostini is a legend around here, and he's also just a really nice guy. When I asked him what his idea of a perfect order at The Hitching Post II is, he was happy to oblige.

Type: Steakhouse, BBQ
Neighborhood: Buellton
Price: $$–$$$
Try the: Grilled Artichoke, Rib Eye, Wine Tasting
Great for: Dates, Wine Excursions, Family Celebrations

64

Left: Meet Frank Ostini, the man, the myth, the legend behind The Hitching Post II. Photo by Jeremy Ball

Center: Meats are cooked on the indoor barbecue using native red oak. Photo by Lisa Thompson

Right: The Angus rib chop might be big enough to share (but it's worth keeping all to yourself). Photo by Lisa Thompson

"It's all about food and wine together," Ostini said. "For wine, you should taste a collection of Hitching Post wines—Pinks Dry Rosé, then the Cork Dancer and Highliner Pinot Noirs. For food, start with a group of shared appetizers—grilled artichoke with smoked tomato mayonnaise, pasilla pepper stuffed with homemade goat cheese, and shrimp with grilled corn salsa. Then the mixed local greens tossed with blue cheese. The entrée would have to be beef. I choose the natural rib eye steak for its amazing flavor, with hand-cut french fries fired three times in beef lard. If there's room, the key lime pie. If there's more room, the old-fashioned chocolate cake."

About that wine he mentioned, The Hitching Post has also produced its own wines made from Central Coast grapes since 1984. Winemaking occurs just a mile from the restaurant, and winery tours are available. You can taste all the Hitching Post wines at the restaurant bar before 6 p.m. for a nominal fee.

406 East Highway 246, Buellton
805-688-0676
hitchingpost2.com

IL FUSTINO

"Il fustino" means "the tank" in Italian, and that's exactly what you'll see when you walk in—rows of gleaming tanks, filled with the best oils and vinegars in town. The staff here encourages you to taste from the source, so you can sample as much as you like and know exactly what you're getting. Once you've made your selections, your purchases are packaged in glass bottles that can be refilled on your next visit.

But choosing, that's the hard part. Il Fustino's cold-pressed extra virgin olive oils are excellent. And so are their flavored oils because the fruit and herbs are crushed right along with the olives, resulting in intense flavors that don't dissipate over time. And the vinegars! You can eat their aged balsamic poured over vanilla ice cream; it's that decadent.

The shelves here aren't limited to oils and vinegar. Il Fustino also sells pantry items like salts, rubs, and pastas.

Il Fustino has a second location downtown in the Santa Barbara Public Market. That one is convenient for snacking—Corazón Cocina is right across the walkway—but this shop is within walking distance of Via Maestra 42, and that's pretty good too.

3401 State St.
805-845-3521
ilfustino.com

Left: You can taste Il Fustino oils straight out of the tank.

Right: The refillable bottles make great hostess gifts.

Type: Pantry Goods
Neighborhood: Upper State
Price: $-$$
Try the: Aged Balsamic, Ascolana EVOO, Smoked Olive Oil
Great for: Housewarmings, Hostess Gifts, Foodies

INDUSTRIAL EATS

Industrial Eats isn't in Santa Barbara proper. It's kind of a drive. About thirty to forty minutes from downtown, actually. But if you really love food and no one told you about this place and you found out about it later, you would be furious. This is the kind of place chefs go to eat. And winemakers. In fact, I don't know that I've ever been to Industrial Eats without seeing at least one or the other there, and I have been an embarrassing number of times.

Housed in a funky warehouse-type space, this casual restaurant grew out of a successful catering business. Owners Jeff and Janet Olsson ran New West Catering in a space next door before deciding to open a restaurant in 2013. Now the restaurant is so popular that they've had to cut back on the catering side of things.

You'll know you're at the right place if you see a large cow statue out front. His name may or may not be Ferdinand; everyone just calls him Cow. When Industrial Eats opened, a lot of spaces nearby were, well, industrial. But now other tasty businesses have sprung up around it, including a winery, brewery, and distillery.

The restaurant is set up like this: there is a long deli counter with an inevitable line to your right, some books and pantry goods on shelves to your left, and a collection of shared tables in the middle. And at the back is the kitchen, anchored by two big dome-shaped ovens. That's where all the magic happens.

Industrial Eats's menu is an ever-changing roster of local delicacies. It's updated so frequently that you can't find an accurate version printed anywhere. It's written out on butcher paper. There is a list of pizzas, another of sandwiches, and a third highlights "Four Words" dishes that have four primary ingredients. Handwritten "86" signs are

Type: New American
Neighborhood: Buellton
Price: $$
Try the: Daily Specials, Pizza, Oysters
Great for: Lunch, Dinner, Picnics

Top left: Industrial Eats is not the place to be stingy when ordering. Try everything!

Top right: Start your eating adventure with an oyster topped with local uni and caviar. Photo by Aron Ives

Above left: Keep your eyes on the ever-changing specials along the counter.

Above right: Definitely order something from the pizza menu to share. Pizzas are fired in two dome-shaped ovens at the back of the restaurant.

taped up as dishes sell out. And there are even more daily specials on clipboards that line the counter.

On a recent visit, I had oysters topped with avocado and caviar, a perfectly garlicky Caesar, chanterelle mushrooms in a cream sauce, and a rosemary, parmesan, and sea salt pizza.

Local wines and a couple of beers are on tap to pair with your meal. Wine is served in a juice glass. It feels kind of like you're being healthy, or maybe you're a winemaker just in from checking on the vineyard.

While many visitors choose to eat in the restaurant, you should know that Industrial Eats can also help you make an incredible picnic or meal at home. Grab a fresh baguette with some preserves and cheese and don't forget to check out the fully stocked butcher case.

181 Industrial Way, Buellton
805-688-8807
industrialeats.com

INTERMEZZO

If you're in the mood for something good but don't know what to choose—perhaps you're hungry, but your date isn't, or you want wine, but your companion wants a cocktail—Intermezzo is the answer to all of your problems.

Want to sit inside? Great, you can choose to belly up to the bar, sit at a table, or lounge by the romantic fire. Prefer relaxing al fresco? Well, there's a front patio if you want to people watch or a back patio with a lovely fountain.

Fancy a glass of wine? Or perhaps a bottle but can't commit? Intermezzo serves up local wines on tap, so you can have as much or as little as you want. But if you feel like something stronger, the bartenders here make a mean manhattan.

And the regional, wine-country-inspired menu is satisfying, whether you choose to indulge in only an appetizer or an entire meal. You might see Intermezzo listed as "American tapas" online, and I think that's accurate. You can share some ahi tartare, dip into a jar of duck confit, and then split a flatbread topped with grilled chicken and peanut sauce. Or you can go whole hog and order fresh ground Wagyu and Angus beef burgers or a grilled New York steak.

It's really up to you at Intermezzo, and that's the best thing about it.

819 Anacapa St.
805-966-9463
intermezzosb.com

Top right: Wagyu and Angus beef burgers are served with housemade pickles.

Above left: It's a nice spot to stop for a cocktail just off State Street.

Above right: Intermezzo's tap wine system keeps wine by the glass fresh and flowing.

Type: Californian
Neighborhood: Downtown
Price: $$
Try the: Cocktails, Burgers, Cheese Plates
Great for: Date Night, Bar Dining, Nightcaps

JANE

If you were on vacation in Santa Barbara and you stumbled across Jane, you would be thrilled. It's a cute sort of place with an exciting but not too crazy menu in easy walking distance from downtown theaters, galleries, and shopping. There is a fireplace, the servers wear crisp white shirts, and you'll likely order something with avocado on it.

Named after the grandmother who encouraged the owners to open their first restaurant—the Montecito Cafe—Jane is a testament to comfortable, quality dining as exemplified by kind service and delectable family recipes.

From a local's perspective, it's also a great place to go for a reliable lunch or to bring a group of potentially picky eaters. If you don't know whether your dining companions like spicy or ethnic foods, Jane is a safe bet.

Jane's menu offers up a little bit of everything, from entrée-sized salads and burgers to delicate linguine with clams. Desserts are incredible here; the coconut cake often sells out. Small, intimate tables dot the venue, with some fireside and balcony seating available. An upstairs room accommodates busy nights and can be reserved for private parties.

Type: Californian
Neighborhood: Downtown
Price: $$
Try the: Trout Salad, Linguine & Clams, Coconut Cake
Great for: Double Dates, Parental Dinners, Private Events

Left: Love a big salad? Jane's got them!

Right: The "Nam" grilled salmon sandwich is served with shaved carrots, cucumber, cilantro, and Sriracha mayonnaise on a homemade bun.

If you're of a social nature and dining alone, or perhaps your group likes a little excitement, opt to sit at the centrally located communal table. You never know whom you'll meet!

1311 State St.
805-962-1311
janerestaurantsb.com

JESSICA FOSTER CONFECTIONS

Chocolatier Jessica Foster began experimenting with truffles in 2001, making chocolates flavored with local delicacies like fresh oranges and lavender as gifts. These were—unsurprisingly—well received, and today you'll still find her at the Santa Barbara Certified Famers Market scouting for seasonal fruits and herbs to include in her creations.

Foster's truffles and other confections are all lovingly made by hand right here in town. Her chocolates are delicious and sold in dozens of stores, as well as stocked at some of the best wineries and hotels in Santa Barbara.

Think chocolate is best enjoyed on its own? Think again. Foster is an expert at pairing chocolate with wines, and not just red wine like you may expect. "People tend to think red wine is the only chocolate pairing success. But I would almost say that white wines are easier to pair," she said. "I've done the Chardonnay Symposium several times and found that the most Chard-friendly truffles are white chocolate coconut, milk chocolate honey almond, white chocolate rose, and white chocolate green tea."

Type: Chocolate
Price: $
Try the: White Chocolate Meyer Lemon Truffle, Sea Salt Caramels, Dark Chocolate Ancho-Cumin Truffle

Left: Jessica Foster herself, hard at work creating sweet treats. Photo by Mega Sorel Photography

Right: Her gorgeous truffles pair beautifully with wine and are available in a number of specialty shops around town.

Want to try the very best one? Although everyone's tastes vary, Foster asserted, "My white chocolate Meyer lemon truffle has always been the most popular. Hands down." But if you want to try the expert's pick, she leans toward the dark chocolate rosemary truffle, which I also think is delicious—not too sweet, with the perfect earthiness.

805-637-6985
jessicafosterconfections.com

KANALOA SEAFOOD

For fish feasts you can feel good about, take a trip to Kanaloa Seafood. Created in 1983 by Don and Randee Disraeli, Kanaloa is committed to supporting and promoting sustainable, environmentally sound fishing practices. In fact, it is the only seafood company in North America to receive the prestigious environmental management certification from the International Organization of Standardization, recognizing the Disraelis' continual pursuit of increasingly ecologically and environmentally sound practices throughout every aspect of their business.

What a reassuring mouthful, right? Well, in addition to being environmentally conscious, Kanaloa is a fun place to shop for—and eat—fish!

Conveniently located in pretty much the dead center of downtown, this business has two facets accessible to the public: the fish market and the restaurant. Both share the same space and are open Monday through Saturday every week. (There is also a wholesale operation that is available to restaurants and retailers.)

The market allows you to choose the freshest fish and shellfish to bring home and cook. You'll find local catches as well as sustainably sourced fish from other areas and hard-to-find items like Spanish octopus, live whelks, and specialty lobsters. Kanaloa's market offers home delivery if you prefer. If you get home delivery, though, you'll miss squeezing in a visit to the restaurant for a snack!

Type: Seafood/Fishmonger
Neighborhood: Downtown
Price: $$
Try the: Fish Taco Sampler, Fishwich, Old Bay Potato Chips
Great for: Happy Hour, Quick Bites, Casual Dinners

Top left: Grab chowder in a bread bowl at this restaurant and fish market.

Above left: Try a fishwich with beer-battered, grilled, or blackened fish and a side of Old Bay potato chips.

Above right: The Baja fish tacos are good too.

The restaurant is a casual place to tuck into tacos, sandwiches, and other fish specialties like ahi poke salad and blackened salmon Caesars. While the menu does have the expected Baja-style fish tacos, it also has some unexpected varieties, including jerk spiced albacore and Korean-inspired salmon and kimchi. Carb-conscious diners can skip the corn tortillas and get their tacos served in lettuce cups instead. And there's an oyster raw bar that makes for perfect appetizers.

If you want to eat here but not everyone in your party loves seafood, don't fret. Kanaloa serves a burger that isn't made from fish at all! In fact, it's a brisket/chuck blend that's topped with melted provolone and served with all the fixings, including housemade Old Bay potato chips. The potato chips are pretty delicious, so you might want to order them even if you don't get the burger.

Kanaloa serves beer and wine to go with your meals. There is a daily happy hour too. Since it's located right behind the mall, it's a fun place to stop in for refreshing snacks and beverages that will perk you right up after battling the retail crowds.

715 Chapala St.
805-966-5159
kanaloaseafood.com

LA CHAPALA MARKET

Some people like eating at Whole Foods. Heck, I do. The idea of eating lunch in a grocery store isn't so weird, is it? After all, the ingredients are right there just waiting to be cooked.

This is kind of similar to that, except there are far fewer organic greens and way more hot, fried tortilla chips. If that appeals to you, dear reader, read on.

At La Chapala Market, you'll find a delicious and fairly priced Mexican restaurant occupying the front of a well-stocked neighborhood market. Until recently, the large sign suspended above the counter was written only in Spanish. That was my first clue that it would be delicious.

The menu includes burritos, tortas, tacos, and sopes. There are breakfast classics too, most served all day. The breakfast burritos are sturdy, and the chilaquiles, well, they're some of the best in town. Both red and green varieties are available with your choice of egg, and the chips are cooked fresh for every order. They won't even make them for you if they suspect the oil is stale. (My second clue!) Beans and diced potatoes strewn with lardons are served on the side, all for around $8.

A meal like this is likely to inspire a powerful thirst. Treat yourself to a housemade horchata or the agua fresca flavor of the week. Last time I went, it was papaya!

5780 Hollister Ave., Goleta
805-681-0277

Type: Mexican
Neighborhood: Goleta
Price: $
Try the: Chilaquiles, Breakfast Burritos, Aguas Frescas
Great for: Lunch, Takeout, Grocery Shopping

Top left: This unassuming corner market in Goleta is home to a delicious Mexican restaurant.

Top right: The menu is long, with affordable tacos and some breakfast dishes available all day.

Above left: The housemade aguas frescas change all the time. This one is papaya.

Above right: La Chapala makes probably the best chilaquiles—green or red—in town, using only freshly fried tortillas.

LA SUPER-RICA TAQUERIA

This wouldn't be a Santa Barbara restaurant guidebook without an entry for this much-beloved, somewhat-contested local favorite. Before we delve into why I 100 percent believe La Super-Rica Taqueria deserves the hype, here's the scoop:

It's pretty hard to have a discussion about La Super-Rica without hearing that it was cooking legend Julia Child's favorite place to eat in Santa Barbara. It's true. She even mentioned it to the whole country on *Good Morning America* once.

That's a pretty intimidating reputation to live up to, so there are some very vocal people for whom it falls short. And admittedly, there are some drawbacks to La Super-Rica. They only take cash, always have a line, and don't serve rice and beans or other similarly kid-friendly entry-level Mexican food dishes. And it's basically a shack, so it's not fancy or romantic in the classic sense.

Don't let any of that stop you from going.

While you won't find ambience and designer flatware, you will find a wonderful, family-run eatery where the tortillas are expertly made by hand while you watch. There's a simple menu where you order by the dish number and, while the tacos are perfectly fine, the specialty dishes are better. The chorizo especial is a warm and wonderful cheese and spicy sausage dish, and the rajas are unlike any other I've tried in the United States or Mexico.

During the week, a changing signboard gives you opportunities to try the tamal de verduras, chile relleno de queso con crema, and chilaquiles, among others. Specials almost always sell out, so if something catches your eye, don't miss your chance to order it.

Type: Mexican
Neighborhood: Eastside
Price: $
Try the: #6, #16, Tamale & Chilaquile Specials
Great for: Lunch, Dinner, Food Photos

Top right: Pay attention and order like a pro using just the number of each dish.

Above left: Dishes are small, so be sure to try a few. Seen here: #2, #6, #13, #18, and #20.

Above right: This little aqua-trimmed shack usually has a line snaking around the block.

Now that you understand what this restaurant is all about, I've got some pro tips to help you have the best trip possible:

- Bring $40 per person. You won't need it—dishes range from $3 to maybe $8—but you'll feel more comfortable.
- Arrive at an unusual hour, preferably on a weekday. Try eating at 11 on Tuesday or 3:30 on Thursday so you don't get stuck waiting in a line that wraps around the block.
- Order the #6. No matter what. Don't usually like rajas? Hate peppers? Doesn't matter. (Unless you're lactose intolerant. There is cheese. Plenty of it.)

And that's basically all there is to it. Oh! You should also make sure your phone battery is charged. You don't want your perfect visit to Julia Child's favorite restaurant in Santa Barbara to go undocumented.

622 North Milpas St.
805-963-4940

THE LARK

Located in the heart of the food- and wine-loving Funk Zone, The Lark is a foodie favorite in Santa Barbara. It was one of the first places to bring higher-end dining to this neighborhood when it opened in 2013, and it's still going strong with great food and a good crowd six nights a week. The seasonal menu celebrates Central Coast ingredients and changes with what's fresh, and you'll definitely see more than one local farm on the roster.

The space itself, designed by Doug Washington, owner of the acclaimed Town Hall and Salt House restaurants in San Francisco, is somehow both warm and industrial.

A mix of new, vintage, and repurposed materials blends together to create both intimate and shared interior and exterior dining spaces. Huddle into a high-walled booth, catch some sun on the spacious patio, or make new friends at the live-edge communal bar table. The wood and metal décor is refreshingly non-Mediterranean.

The unique industrial feel is just what owner Sherry Villanueva was going for. "Why open The Lark in the Funk Zone? The Funk Zone is the neighborhood where locals love to come because it's original, creative, and fun," said Villanueva. "Our neighborhood celebrates so many things we love about Santa Barbara: home of the Urban Wine Trail, adjacent to the ocean and the heart of downtown, and the epicenter of Santa Barbara's creative community. We also love being in an historic district that celebrates Santa Barbara's industrial past."

Chef Jason Paluska has created a menu composed of snacks; farm, ranch, and sea dishes; and platters. Most dishes are intended for sharing and are served family style, especially the grander-sized

Type: New American
Neighborhood: Funk Zone
Price: $$–$$$
Try the: Seasonal Cocktails, Brussels Sprouts,
Grilled Octopus
Great for: Outdoor Dining, Bar Dining, Special Occasions

Top left: The Lark is a hip, dinner-only destination in the Funk Zone. Photo by Erin Feinblatt

Top right: Chef Jason Paluska turns out seasonal dishes that celebrate the bounty of the Central Coast, like this summer special of pork belly and stone fruit. Photo by Rob Stark

Above left: Looking for low carb options? Try the marinated and grilled hanger steak with charred broccoli and crispy shallots. Photo by Rob Stark

Above right: Don't forget to save room for dessert! The Lark's banana cream and hibiscus bowl is shown here. Photo by Rob Stark

platters. "I like to start my evening by choosing a platter and working my way backwards through the other parts of the menu," Villanueva shared. "The platter can set the stage for the evening, and it's fun to build a full dinner around other dishes that complement it."

Menu items you might try when you visit include lamb sirloin tartare with crumbled niçoise olives and sheep's milk feta, grilled Spanish octopus with toasted faro and tangelo marmalade, and smoked foie gras torchon with spiced pistachios and grilled olive sourdough. And crisp Brussels sprouts with Medjool dates, always the Brussels sprouts. "This signature dish is so popular we can never take them off the menu."

The Lark has a perfectly curated cocktail list as well as a healthy selection of beer and wines. Les Marchands, a wine bar in the same restaurant family, is right around the corner with pretty much every vintage you could ever want (and more great food too).

131 Anacapa St.
805-284-0370
thelarksb.com

LILAC PATISSERIE

Beautifully designed with cases of well-lit, tantalizing, and wheat-free baked goods, Lilac Patisserie is the bakery that gluten-free dreams are made of! Owned and operated by husband-and-wife pastry chefs Alam and Gillian Muralles, this State Street eatery is dedicated to serving cakes, tarts, sandwiches, and more that are completely gluten free.

Open for breakfast, lunch, and dessert all week, Lilac Patisserie's menus run the gamut from toast and quiche of the day to chicken salad sandwiches and seasonal pies. The fruit tarts are quite lovely, and everything is presented nicely, owing largely to Gillian's cake decorating background.

Lilac Patisserie also does a brisk business in custom cake orders, with beautifully decorated cakes that are light and fluffy. For anyone with wheat sensitivities, the range of flavors available here is a nice change of pace from the more limited options you typically find elsewhere. Think coconut cream, chocolate sea salt caramel, and peanut butter meringue, among others. Vegan cakes are available too.

Of course, whether you decide to eat in or take your order to go, your food will taste equally delightful. But there's something to be said about Lilac's bright State Street location. It's close to shopping, movies, and other attractions and great for photos!

1017 State St.
805-845-7400
lilacpatisserie.com

Type: Bakery/Cafe
Neighborhood: Downtown
Price: $-$$
Try the: Lemon Blueberry Tart, Quiche, Berry Patch Cake
Great for: Gluten-Free, Breakfast, Dessert

These tarts are all sweet, no wheat. Photo by Aron Ives

LILLY'S TAQUERIA

I don't know if you're into cheek tacos. Or eyeball or brain or tongue tacos. But if you are, I know where you should go.

For the most authentic tacos in Santa Barbara, head to Lilly's. Unobtrusively tucked in an out-of-the-way shopping center at the oceany end of downtown, Lilly's Taqueria has been serving up sizzling meats on soft corn tortillas to lines of customers for years.

There are no chips, no rice, and nary a bean in sight...just tacos. For around $2 a pop, you can choose from a variety of meats, including asada, adobada, and even ojos. Yep, you read that right! Lilly's proudly offers a variety of less-common taco fillings. Some tortillas are grilled, some are steamed, but they're all soft. And corn.

And yes, they do have a vegetarian taco for your meat-abstaining friends and family members. It's not great, but it's fine.

Order a few, then hit the salsa bar to dress them up with freshly made salsa, lime, cilantro, and radish before scarfing them down! Jarritos and Mexican Cokes are available should you feel parched.

(It may seem like I'm underselling this place, but I just don't want too many people to go. The line is already long enough.)

310 Chapala St.
805-966-9180
lillystacos.com

Top left: Lilly's authentic street tacos are packed with meat.

Above left: The steamed tripas taco is served only on weekends and is melt-in-your-mouth soft.

Above right: Here's a peek at the menu to help you plan your order.

Type: Taqueria
Neighborhood: Downtown
Price: $
Try the: Tripas Con Leche, Cachete, Carne Asada
Great for: Carnivores, Anyone with $5

THE FRENCH PRESS Try a warm apple Danish, made fresh in the bakeshop right next door.

ARIGATO SUSHI Freshwater eel nigiri.

THE BLUE OWL Owner and chef Cindy Black stocks her restaurant with great eats and local wines. *Photo by Willhouse Photography*

BOUCHON In the fall, you might try this goat cheese tart with pecan crust, herbed chèvre, persimmons, frisée, and pomegranate gastrique. *Photo by Shelly Vinson Photography*

DUTCH GARDEN Inside it's a dark haven of beer, taxidermy, and garden gnomes.

C'EST CHEESE Start your day off right with a gourmet breakfast grilled cheese at C'est Cheese. *Photo by Lindsey Baumsteiger*

LILAC PATISSERIE Lilac Patisserie serves gluten-free breakfast, lunch, and dessert.

EMPTY BOWL GOURMET NOODLE BAR Start your meal with the green papaya salad at Empty Bowl Noodle Bar.

LUCKY'S This steak, chops, and seafood destination is located on a popular shopping street.

OLIO GUCINA Olio Crudo's polipo dish is a cold mix of Mediterranean octopus, sliced new potatoes, frisée, and Controne pepper. *Photo by Gary Moss*

ON THE ALLEY Shown here: one fried fish taco and one fried avocado taco.

PARADISE CAFE Steamed local mussels are available depending on the season.

SAMA SAMA KITCHEN A rich dish of roasted Kurobuta pork belly, black pepper-leek rice porridge, organic sunny side up egg, soy, sesame oil, and garlic crackers. *Photo by Cara Robbins*

SLY'S Head to Sly's for French fare like these moules et frites.

YOICHI'S For the fifth course, mushimono, you will have your choice of steamed and simmered dishes, which may include oysters steamed in a citrus bowl. *Photo by Aron Ives*

GA'DARIO Grilled rack of lamb with shaved garlic pairs nicely with hearty local wine.

LITO'S MEXICAN RESTAURANT

At first glance, this maybe isn't the kind of restaurant you expect to be sent to by a guidebook. I get it. The façade isn't fancy, and the seating area has kind of a cafeteria aesthetic. But trust me, it's delicious.

Open every day from 6:30 a.m. to 4 p.m., this family-run eatery serves up amazing breakfast burritos, delicious enchiladas, savory soups, and much, much more. Order at the counter, take a seat, and enjoy some chips and homemade salsa while you wait. It won't be long, and the staff is very friendly.

Lito's is a Santa Barbara local secret. Or at least it was until 2011 when Guy Fieri visited and featured it on *Diners, Drive-Ins and Dives*. Guy liked the flavor of the carnitas, which can be ordered in a taco, burrito, enchilada, or torta. The pozole, a pork stew you top with cabbage, cilantro, and lime, also impressed Guy. And now sometimes there's a line out the door!

I personally love their enchiladas—the red sauce is killer—and I've never seen my husband order anything other than the Chile Colorado Burrito. He's an adventurous eater who devours everything under the sun, from sweetbreads to sea urchin, so if that isn't a solid recommendation, I don't know what is.

514 East Haley St.
805-962-1559
litosmexfoodsb.com

Left: Lito's sign lets you know that Guy Fieri ate here for an episode of *Diners, Drive-Ins and Dives*.

Right: Fill up on giant burritos. Chips and homemade salsa come free with every meal.

Type: Mexican
Neighborhood: Eastside
Price: $
Try the: Chile Colorado, Carnitas, Enchiladas
Great for: Families, Breakfast, Lunch, Hangovers

LOQUITA

A relative newcomer to the Santa Barbara restaurant scene, Loquita seems to have already found its footing as the local destination for Spanish-inspired dishes. With a warm interior, inviting bar, spacious patio, and brightly colored tiles throughout, this is exactly the kind of place you want to visit when you're on a seaside vacation. If you're lucky enough to live here, so much the better.

Loquita is the most recent venture by Acme Hospitality, the same brand behind The Lark, Lucky Penny, and others. This restaurant brings Spanish flavors and traditional cooking methods stateside, with hot and cold tapas, wood-fired seafood, grilled meats, and three types of paella. The menu feels right at home here in the pseudo-Mediterranean climate. Nothing is too heavy, but there are plenty of hot, spiced dishes that can warm you up when a cool breeze is blowing.

Executive chef Peter Lee has created a menu that is both exotic and approachable. There are familiar tapas and charcuterie mixed with harder-to-find dishes like Spanish octopus with black garlic aioli and chicken croquettes. The three paellas—land, sea, and vegetarian—make perfect dishes to share, and churros with an assortment of dipping sauces round out your meal nicely.

The full bar is delicious. Cocktails are a little pricier perhaps, but when you see the craftsmanship and ingredients that go into each, you will be won over. At least four different kinds of gin and tonics are available. The Maravilloso G&T is probably my favorite, garnished with pink peppercorns and a sprig of rosemary.

Brunch is served on Sundays and may or may not include flamenco dance performances by some of Santa Barbara's leading Old Spanish Days dancers. For the best seat, you'll want to call ahead and reserve a place on the patio. If it's chilly, ask to be seated near the fireplace,

Type: Spanish
Neighborhood: Funk Zone
Price: $$-$$$
Try the: Pulpo, Mariscos Paella, Churros
Great for: Brunch, Tapas, Cocktails

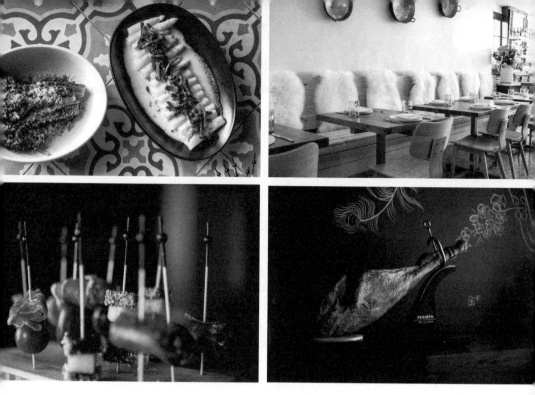

Top left: Loquita puts on a beautiful spread in Santa Barbara's Funk Zone. Photo by Rob Stark

Top right: The interior is light and bright, with paella dishes decorating the wall. Photo by Rob Stark

Above left: It's hard to say no to pintxos, small finger foods that pack a big flavor. Photo by Rob Stark

Above right: It wouldn't be a Spanish restaurant without a ham leg perched up somewhere. Photo by Rob Stark

which is lined with colorful sardine tins. The brunch menu has a mix of classics with a Spanish twist. The croissant is filled with chorizo, manchego, and soft scrambled eggs, and the Benedict is topped with serrano ham and spicy hollandaise.

Tucked around the corner at the back of the restaurant is Poquito, its little sister walk-up counter and takeaway with a focus on pintxos. Pintxos are small bar snacks, often served on toothpicks or skewers. You can also get tuna bocadillos (Spanish sandwiches), wild mushroom cocas (kind of like flatbreads), and cheese plates too. If you choose to eat in, you have the option of washing down your order with a lager, glass of spicy red wine, or Spanish vermouth.

202 State St.
805-880-3380
loquitasb.com

LOS AGAVES

When the first Los Agaves opened on Milpas in 2008, I thought, "Great, another Mexican restaurant. Just what we needed."

Flash forward almost ten years, and I'm more than ready to admit that I was wrong. Los Agaves filled a void I didn't realize existed. It's not your local taqueria, and it's not a fancy sit-down Mexican restaurant concept. Los Agaves fits somewhere in between. It's casual and comfortable with good food and reasonable prices.

Owner Carlos Luna created a menu that is familiar and unique all at once. You can pop in for classic favorites like nachos, chiles rellenos, and fajitas. Or you can try something a little more unusual such as mole enchiladas and molcajetes, a tomato stew full of cactus, onions, peppers, and your choice of protein served boiling in a scalding hot lava rock bowl.

Being located in a beach community, Los Agaves serves a wide variety of seafood dishes too. Because fish and shrimp are best served fresh, you'll find the tastiest dishes listed on the specials board, which is updated daily. You might see ahi tuna ceviche one day and seared sea bass on coconut rice the next. The grilled salmon tacos are excellent, never fishy and always served with chunks of grilled pineapple.

Although the three locations serve the same menu—and there's another location in Westlake—each one has its own feel. Goleta is clean and modern, packed with students and corporate employees on the weekdays. De La Vina is tucked in a residential neighborhood and draws a lot of families. Milpas, mentioned earlier, is the original location and has one huge advantage: it serves breakfast on the weekends too.

Whichever location you choose, you're sure to feel right at home. "At Los Agaves, we have always taken tremendous pride in being a part of

Type: Mexican
Neighborhood: Downtown, Upper State, Goleta
Price: $-$$
Try the: Nachos, Molcajetes, Mole Enchiladas
Great for: Families, Students, Groups

Top left: You'll often see Los Agaves owner Carlos Luna working in one of his restaurants.

Top right: The kitchen is always busy at every location.

Above left: A varied menu means there's something for everyone at this beloved Mexican restaurant.

Above right: Adventurous eaters should order the molcajetes, a tomato-based dish served boiling hot in a lava rock bowl.

the community, embracing our neighboring businesses and residents alike," said Luna.

It's that attitude that has won Los Agaves legions of local fans. It is frequently voted both best Mexican restaurant and best salsa in Santa Barbara polls. The enthusiasm appears to be spreading too. In 2016, it was named #16 on Yelp's Top 100 Places to Eat in the US.

600 North Milpas St.
805-564-2626

2911 De La Vina St.
805-682-2600

7024 Market Place Dr., Goleta
805-968-4000

los-agaves.com

111

LUCKY PENNY

What's got great pizza, a convenient location, and 164,456 pennies covering the walls? If you answered Lucky Penny, you're right!

This beacon of a restaurant is tiled with real copper pennies. It can't be spotted from State Street, but if you're in the Funk Zone it's hard to miss. Brought to you by Acme Hospitality—the Funk Zone food and beverage powerhouse brand behind The Lark, Loquita, Les Marchands, Santa Barbara Wine Collective, and Helena Avenue Bakery—the Lucky Penny is your go-to for wood-fired pizza, sandwiches, and salads.

A wood-burning oven churns out thin-crust pizzas all week long, starting at 11 a.m. The menu here is anything but basic. If you're hoping for a simple cheese or meat lovers' pie, you're out of luck. If, however, you're craving a pizza topped with fingerling potatoes, chorizo, spicy tomatillo marinara, cotija, cilantro, and a fried egg, then this is the place.

The most popular pizza at Lucky Penny is the Parker, which is made with roasted wild mushrooms, rosemary, mozzarella, and parmesan. This pizza is named after Parker Gumins, a local kid who came closest to guessing the total number of pennies glued to the outside of the building. His prize was to design a pizza and host a big pizza party with all his friends.

While pizza is the top seller here, salads and hot and cold sandwiches are available as well. You might try the Lucky Penny cold brew coffee pulled pork sammy served on brioche or opt for something healthier like the shaved kale salad.

Type: Pizza
Neighborhood: Funk Zone
Price: $$
Try the: Frosé, LP Classic Pizza, Milpas Pizza
Great for: Lunch, Wine Drinkers, Photo Ops

Top left: This place is known for wood-fired pizzas in the Funk Zone. Photo by Rob Stark

Above left: You can also get salads and sandwiches, like this meatball sub. Photo by Rob Stark

Above right: Lucky Penny isn't hard to find. Just look for the building covered in 164,456 pennies. Photo by Erin Feinblatt

Whatever you decide to order, it's fun to eat onsite at one of the picnic tables on the garden-style patio, but be warned: seats fill up quickly, particularly on nice days (and aren't almost all of them nice here in beautiful Santa Barbara?) The good news, you can also take your pizza into almost any of the many wineries within walking distance and enjoy it there. If you happen to be enjoying a beer across the way at Figueroa Mountain Brewing Co., the friendly Lucky Penny staff will bring it right to you.

One more fun thing about this hip pizza joint is that you can place your order online via the website for pick-up or to eat in. Ideal for when you're craving pizza but in a rush or feeling antisocial. It's super simple!

127 Anacapa St.
805-284-0358
luckypennysb.com

LUCKY'S

Self-proclaimed as "Montecito's second living room," Lucky's is a classic steakhouse with a relaxed Old Hollywood feel. Operated by the Montesano Group—led by Gene Montesano of Lucky Brand Jeans fame—it's where you go to dine with affluent and sometimes celebrity meat lovers in a sophisticated setting. You might recognize a few of your fellow diners from the local paper, the *Wall Street Journal*, or *Entertainment Weekly*. If you do, you'll act like you don't because that's what we do here in Santa Barbara.

Given to impeccable preparation of basic dishes, Lucky's is a steaks, chops, and seafood place. Aged Midwestern USDA Prime beef in a variety of cuts draws rave reviews, as do racks of lamb, chops, Maine lobster, fresh fish, and hefty shrimp cocktails. Meats are served on their own, and you order sides that complement your entrée choice. You might try sautéed mushrooms, traditional fresh creamed corn, or hashed brown potatoes with Gruyère cheese. Terrific ingredients make the difference, and everything is whipped up in-house, from the dressings to the corned beef hash. Oh wait, did I mention they serve brunch?

Brunch is an underpublicized delight here. Served only on weekends from 9 a.m. to 3 p.m., the menu has a lot of traditional items like eggs Benedict, brioche french toast, and a mixed vegetable frittata, but it holds some surprises too. You can start your day with an open-faced filet mignon sandwich, matzo ball soup, or local abalone. And it's not uncommon to be treated to a free mimosa or two while you're there.

Type: Steakhouse
Neighborhood: Montecito
Price: $$$
Try the: Escargots, New York Strip Steak, Onion Strings
Great for: Cocktails, Dinner, People Watching

Left: Steak? Sole? Whatever you choose, don't forget to order onion strings on the side.

Right: Settle in for steak dinner in "Montecito's living room."

On the topic of drinks, Lucky's bar is fabulous. Get a proper martini, a manhattan, a Tom Collins . . . it's the right atmosphere for sipping a strong, boozy beverage, and the bartenders know just how to make what you like.

Things aren't inexpensive at Lucky's (you can get a $27 salad!), but you don't expect them to be, given the posh setting and usually fantastic service. The stylish interior boasts black-and-white photos of classic film stars, and an outdoor patio adds charm on warm summer nights.

Although Lucky's is always a popular destination for celebratory dinners and special events, you don't have to be rich to join in the fun. Sit at the bar, rub elbows with Santa Barbara's who's who, and order a plate of onion strings and a martini—now that's an evening well spent!

1279 Coast Village Rd.
805-565-7540
luckys-steakhouse.com

MCCONNELL'S FINE ICE CREAMS

McConnell's Fine Ice Creams is pretty sweet, in terms of both taste and Santa Barbara history. Way back in 1949, local husband-and-wife team Gordon "Mac" and Ernesteen McConnell decided to start an ice cream company that would do things differently. In a time when food processes were being mechanized, they sourced ingredients like milk, cream, fruits, nuts, and produce from Central Coast farms and purveyors. They made their own jams and baked their own cookies and other inclusions so that everything was made in house, from start to finish.

Inevitably, Santa Barbara fell in love with McConnell's Fine Ice Creams, queuing up at every opportunity, even as the brand passed from one family to the next and then the next over a period of decades. Most recently, Santa Barbara husband and wife Michael Palmer and Eva Ein took the reins in 2012.

Today, McConnell's ice creams continue to be made completely from scratch at every turn, from pasteurizing local, grass-fed milk to creating the flavor swirls that run through many of their varieties. True to Mac's original dictates, there are still no artificial colors, flavors, or fillers added. The ice cream is made over on Milpas Street at The Old Dairy, built in 1939 and exclusively devoted to ice cream since the 1950s. It's also McConnell's Fine Ice Creams's world headquarters.

Type: Dessert
Neighborhood: Downtown
Price: $
Try the: Churro Con Leche, Salted Caramel Chip, Eureka Lemon & Marionberry
Great for: Kids, Sweet Tooths, Hot Days

Top left: Grab a cone at Santa Barbara's favorite ice cream parlor. Photo by McConnell's Fine Ice Creams

Above left: Find the tastiest ice cream shop right in the middle of downtown. Photo by McConnell's Fine Ice Creams

Above center: Or treat yourself to something a little naughtier, like this s'mores sundae. Photo by McConnell's Fine Ice Creams

Above right: When in doubt, add sprinkles. Photo by McConnell's Fine Ice Creams

The first McConnell's ice cream shop was located at the intersection of Mission and State Street, where Garrett's diner is now. This new location was opened in 2013 and is more convenient to hungry downtown shoppers. So convenient, in fact, that there's usually a line. Even in winter.

The good news about the line is that it moves quickly but gives you a little extra time to figure out your order. You'll certainly need it! In addition to cones and cups, you can get shakes, floats, sundaes, ice cream sandwiches, and affogato. There are cafe tables inside if you choose to eat on premises, or you can just grab a cone and stroll.

The long list of ice cream flavors is anything but standard, with new specials popping up seasonally. You might decide to keep it light with Sweet Cream or indulge in something more decadent like Chocolate Covered Strawberries or Cardamom & Gingersnaps. Not sure which flavor to choose? Get a flight and sample three different ice creams at once.

728 State St.
805-324-4402
mcconnells.com

MESA VERDE

Trying to eat healthier—especially when you're on vacation and dining out for every meal—is no easy feat. Veggie burgers are boring. Salads, well, you can just make them yourself. Why pay someone for a salad? It's no wonder that vegetarians get heckled. In the wrong hands, meat-free meals can be entirely . . . mediocre.

But ask my rather masculine group of meat-loving chef friends to name their favorite restaurants in town, and Mesa Verde will somewhat surprisingly come up again and again. The only animal protein on the menu here is a very scarcely used, completely optional egg, but that doesn't stop them from visiting this Mesa eatery to see what's fresh on the menu.

At Mesa Verde, you'll experience a beautiful (and filling) plant-based cuisine featuring a unique vegan and organic menu with primarily locally harvested ingredients. Head chef Christopher Rayman turns out plates that are as photogenic as they are flavorful.

Try a brunch of potato latkes and tempeh bacon with Pink Lady apples and pea tendrils. At lunch, tuck into picadillo empanadas with cashew cheese and fragrant chimichurri, or enjoy the umami flavors of a pulled smoked mushroom sandwich. Dig into a dinner of polenta fries and street tacos made with jackfruit chorizo. Rayman's innovative menu changes with what's in season, but you can usually find at least a few of these dishes there.

In addition to hearty entrées, Mesa Verde also serves homemade desserts and housemade juices and herbal tonics. Desserts are vegan and gluten-free, but that doesn't mean they're not delicious.

Type: Vegetarian
Neighborhood: Mesa
Price: $$
Try the: Street Tacos, Polenta Fries, Baklava
Great for: Vegans, Vegetarians, Produce Enthusiasts

Top left: This Mesa gem is green through and through. Photo by Curtis Miller

Top right: Vegetarian and vegan eats get expert treatment here by chef Christopher Rayman. Photo by Curtis Miller

Above left: Bring your camera. Seasonal creations are garnished and plated with care. Photo by Curtis Miller

Above right: This beautiful cheese board is actually vegan, featuring dairy-free cashew cheese. Photo by Curtis Miller

People rave about Mesa Verde's baklava! Pair it with Artemis's Brew with raspberry leaf if you're feeling worn down or Kali's Chai for a fragrant, caffeinated pick-me-up.

To sum up: if you really like vegetables, you'll really like Mesa Verde. And if you don't really like vegetables, I'd be willing to bet that you'll also really like Mesa Verde. This restaurant is great for gluten-free diners, vegans, and vegetarians, of course, but even committed meatatarians love coming here for the occasional guilt-free meal.

1919 Cliff Dr.
805-963-4474
mesaverderestaurant.com

METROPULOS

Let's begin with a warning: don't even think about setting foot in this specialty deli unless you are prepared to walk out with a handful of assorted delicacies you didn't even know you needed. That said, if you are the type of person that likes discovering exotic seasonings, buttery cheeses, and unusual European ingredients, this is the lunch stop for you.

Metropulos opened in 2004. It's pretty much the original Funk Zone eatery. And it's the perfect place to pop into before, after, or during a nearby wine tasting.

First things first, head up to the counter to place your order for a fresh salad or decadent sandwich made with luxe ingredients like prosciutto and cranberry-fig confit. And then you are free to browse. The cheese counter, the charcuterie case, the dessert display, the rows and rows of handmade pasta, chocolates . . . all of this is yours to peruse while you wait.

And did we mention the wine cave? Grab a bottle (or half-bottle) of locally made wine to take home or open onsite to enjoy with your meal. Sit inside or grab some sun on the front patio. Just keep in mind that the tables are small and Metropulos operates on a first come, first served principle.

216 East Yanonali St.
805-899-2300
metrofinefoods.com

Top right: Metropulos is a gourmet deli located in Santa Barbara's Funk Zone, just a few blocks from the beach.

Above left: Grab a gyro or made-to-order deli sandwich.

Above right: The shelves inside are stocked with specialty items, like handmade pastas, tinned Spanish fish, and peppers from different regions.

Type: Deli
Neighborhood: Funk Zone
Price: $
Try the: Gyros, Sandwiches, Empanadas
Great for: Casual Lunches, Picnic Supplies

MONY'S MEXICAN FOOD

Mony's Mexican Food is like a super-deluxe taqueria. It has proper street tacos, an epic salsa bar, freshly made chips, and a long menu of non-taco options. The family that runs this business has a heck of a lot of fans too. People come up from LA to eat at Mony's. And it's not like LA is running short of Mexican food restaurants.

There are a few challenges to Mony's. For one, the space is small. There is usually a line, and it's not uncommon to be hard up for a place to sit. Also, the hours are tricky, at least for corporate working stiffs like me. Since Mony's closes every day at 4:30 and is closed Sunday, Saturday is really my only window to pop by, since I don't live in the area. And parking is tricky in the Funk Zone on Saturdays, because wine. Everyone and their mommas head out to this area to visit the wineries on the weekends.

But still I go. That's how good it is. Worth every inconvenience. You can choose from tacos, enchiladas, tortas, burritos, nachos, alambres, and fajitas here. Affordably priced dishes are served with your choice of meat and made fresh while you wait. Meats like asada, al pastor, and tripas are available, as well as fish and shrimp and rajas for our plant-based friends. You can get two tacos for less than $5, and they come mounded with cilantro and onions. There's also a barbacoa beef plate, mole chicken plate, and chilaquiles.

Type: Mexican
Neighborhood: Funk Zone
Price: $
Try the: Al Pastor Tacos, Pistachio Salsa,
Chicken Mole Enchiladas
Great for: Early Lunch, Take Out, Late Afternoon Snacks

Left: Hidden down a side street, Mony's is a small restaurant with a big following. You've got to go early to beat the line on weekends.

Right: Just a light brunch of chilaquiles and mole enchiladas.

If you're a burrito fan—and I am—you'll appreciate the fact that the cooks grill the burritos here, so the tortillas brown on the outside a little. This extra touch adds a depth of flavor to the typically bland wrapper, so it's warm and the flavor blends perfectly with the fillings when you take a bite. You can ask for your burrito well done, and they will leave it on a little longer for you.

The salsa bar is a real crowd-pleaser at Mony's. There are usually eight freshly made salsas for you to choose from, ranging from the more traditional red and green to adventurous pistachio and habanero salsas.

Mony's also has a truck available to cater events. It's perfect for weddings, birthday parties, and fiestas.

217 Anacapa St.
805-895-2978
monyssb.com

THE NATURAL CAFE

Wherever you travel in Santa Barbara, it seems like you're never more than a few miles away from The Natural Cafe. And that's a good thing. This fast casual, healthy spot is a smart choice for a satisfying meal that won't break your budget.

With even more locations in neighboring counties, The Natural Cafe is a Santa Barbara small business success story. A local favorite for vegetarian and vegan options, this popular lunch and dinner restaurant also serves up delicious chicken and fish entrées. In all of their semi-casual establishments, you place your order at the counter and then wait for your food to be delivered to your table.

Popular dishes include their veggie tacos, savory turkey and meatless burgers, and signature Caesar salad generously topped with avocado. The fresh fish tacos are also tasty and a nice change of pace from the fried options available elsewhere.

Save room for dessert while you're here. The dessert case has some tempting options—cakes and cookies mainly—and the made-to-order shakes and smoothies are delicious.

Type: Californian
Neighborhood: Downtown, Uptown Goleta
Price: $
Try the: Local Favorite Sandwich, Fish Tacos, Carrot Shake
Great for: Casual Meals, Family Dining

Left: The State Street favorite is both healthy and affordable.

Right: The aptly named Local's Favorite is an avocado sandwich with garlic mayo, lettuce, tomato, sprouts, and red onion.

508 State St., Santa Barbara
805-962-9494

361 Hitchcock Way, Santa Barbara
805-563-1163

6990 Marketplace Dr., Goleta
805-685-2039

thenaturalcafe.com

Noodle City is a mom-and-pop Vietnamese restaurant located in Old Town Goleta. It is small, busy, loud, and sometimes even a little smoky. When you leave, you might smell a little like a noodle shop. But that's okay. If anything, that's a win because what fun is a sterile, flavorless Vietnamese restaurant?

To no one's surprise, Noodle City serves mainly noodles. It's known for dishing up some of the best pho in the area. Fresh pots of broth are bubbling on the stove in the small kitchen around the clock, and real Thai basil is used as a garnish. They have several varieties, including a vegetarian version, but, heads up, it still uses a beef broth.

Vegetarians have plenty of non-pho options, though. The rest of the menu has crispy noodle plates, vermicelli bowls, wide flat noodle stir-fries, and rice plates. The majority can be made with beef, chicken, pork, shrimp, tofu, soy proteins (e.g., "vegetarian chicken"), or vegetables. The bun bowls are fresh and delicious, with your choice of meat or other topping spread over thin rice vermicelli noodles, with fresh sprouts and other crispy raw veggies and a side of fish sauce. Plant-based diners can opt out of the fish sauce, of course.

The space itself is narrow and typical of other buildings in Old Town Goleta. One side is mirrored, and that's where you'll see the specials taped up. There's a counter at the back for takeout orders. Noodle City is sandwiched between one of the better Asian food markets in the area and a funky beer and wine bar. You can grab some soup, buy some quail eggs, and have a killer draft beer, all in one stop.

Type: Vietnamese
Neighborhood: Goleta
Price: $
Try the: Pho, Bun, Crispy Noodle
Great for: Hungry People, Grownups, Lunch

Left: Find some of the best pho in town in this strip mall in Old Town Goleta.

Right: Mi Xoa Don, crispy noodles with vegetables. Choice of meat or soy protein optional.

Service can be abrupt; some reviewers have even complained that they found the staff rude. That's not true at all. They are very kind, but they do have their own no-nonsense way when it's busy—which is often—so you may feel a little less pandered to than you would at other sit-down restaurants. Just remember: you're there for the food, not the small talk. Students and local professionals eat here regularly. Expect to find it especially packed around lunchtime.

5869 Hollister Ave., Goleta
805-683-6818

NOOK

If you like the idea of food trucks but wish they came with a more permanent address, consistent service, and a seemingly endless supply of beer, you're going to love the Nook.

Operating out of a modified shipping container affixed between two taprooms, Nook serves up affordably priced comfort food in Santa Barbara's Funk Zone. Think burgers, sandwiches, fries, and salads—but with a twist!

Chef Norbert Schulz is one of the better-known chefs in town, having spent decades helming fine dining restaurants in the area. Schulz himself is German, but he and his wife set up shop here more than thirty-five years ago, pretty much on a whim, and they've been part of the local restaurant scene ever since. If you've lived here for a few decades, there's a good chance you've eaten at one of his past locations like Brigitte's and Oyster's.

Now you can eat food made by a fancy chef with a less fancy price tag. Think housemade bratwurst, blackened rockfish tacos, and foie gras burgers, all under $20. Specials change daily, but there is a pretty standard menu that has options for pescatarians, vegetarians, vegans, and gluten-free diners. The grilled salmon salad is sizeable for the price and decked out with local berries, and if you're looking for something really decadent, you should try the lobster mac and cheese. You will see actual chunks of lobster in there.

The kitchen opens every day at 11:30, just in time for lunch. Nook shares a space in the Funk Zone's Waterline project, a large warehouse-style building with multiple vendors. The windows where you order and pick up your food face into Lama Dog Taproom, a taproom with a wide and changing selection of craft beers. You can eat there, sit on

Type: California Comfort Food
Neighborhood: Funk Zone
Price: $$
Try the: Lobster Mac & Cheese, Nook Burger, Bratwurst
Great for: Lunch, Linner, Dinner, Drinking

Top left: Chef Norbert Schulz helms Nook, his most recent local restaurant.

Top right: Like bratwurst? Try Nook's—it's made right here in house.

Above left: The lobster mac and cheese with white truffle butter and garlic croutons is a menu staple.

Above right: This fried chicken sandwich isn't always on the menu, but if you see it on the specials list, you should try it.

the sunny patio with your dog, or cross through the hallway to the other side of the building. There you can choose between Topa Topa, a local brewery, and Fox Wine Co. There's also some retail space in the building for people who like to shop while they eat and drink.

The Funk Zone is a very walkable district of Santa Barbara filled with shops, galleries, restaurants, and tasting rooms, and the Nook is centrally located. The whole area gets busy on weekends—particularly in the summer. If you don't like crowds, try visiting during the week.

116 Santa Barbara St.
805-880-3365
nooksantabarbara.com

NORTON'S PASTRAMI AND DELI

Norton's Pastrami and Deli has long been a locals' favorite. But now, after an appearance on an episode of *Diners, Drive-Ins and Dives*, the secret is out. As the name suggests, if you like pastrami, this lunch-counter-style restaurant is the place to go in Santa Barbara.

What makes it so good here is the large, well-seasoned flat top grill in easy view of the dining space. That's where you can see and hear your pastrami sizzling away, building up your anticipation while your food is made to order. The less traditional Mom's PLT is the crowd favorite, with crispy fried pastrami, chipotle mayo, lettuce, and tomato sandwiched between two slices of sourdough. But the classic pastrami on rye and pastrami dip are lipsmackingly good too.

Norton's has cornered the pastrami market for brunch, lunch, and linner, serving food only between 10:30 a.m. and 3:30 or 4 p.m., and only Monday through Saturday. So the mood had better not strike you on a Sunday.

You don't have to limit yourself to pastrami when you visit, although if it's your first trip you probably should. There's a whole host of meaty goodness for you to explore. They've got corned beef, Philly steaks, and Hebrew National hot dogs done up various ways—including mounded with pastrami.

Norton's also has turkey Reubens and grilled chicken sandwiches if you prefer winged creatures. And for our pescatarian-leaning friends, they have tuna melts (with or without avocado and bacon) and sandwiches.

Type: Deli
Neighborhood: Downtown
Price: $
Try the: Mom's PLT, Reuben, Pastrami Dog
Great for: Lunch, Deli Enthusiasts, Food Network Fans

Top left: Downtown shoppers can refuel at Norton's.

Top right: This pastrami palace was featured on *Diners, Drive-Ins and Dives*.

Above left: Pastrami sizzles on the flat top all day long.

Above right: Everyone loves Mom's PLT (pastrami, lettuce, and tomato with chipotle mayo).

If you don't eat meat and you somehow end up being dragged to Norton's by a well-meaning but carnivorous companion, don't despair! Norton's makes a tasty grilled cheese on toasted sourdough with grilled tomato and onion and truly melty cheese.

And the onion rings and pickles are real people pleasers all around.

Another fun thing about Norton's is that it's located on one of the yummiest side streets of downtown Santa Barbara. It's right next to the oldest bar in the city, The Sportsman, and very close to great Mexican food if you've saved room. But chances are you haven't, so maybe try that next time. There's also killer coffee at The French Press on the corner. A fresh cup of joe might just be what you need to stay awake after eating so much pastrami.

18 West Figueroa St.
805-965-3210
nortonspastrami.com

OLIO CUCINA

This is a family of three fantastic Italian restaurants, all located on the same block in Santa Barbara. See below to discover why each merits its own trip!

Olio e Limone Ristorante—Suite #17

Husband-and-wife team Alberto and Elaine Morello opened this, their first restaurant, in 1999. Their goal was simple: to offer Santa Barbara creative, authentic Italian cuisine served in an inviting atmosphere. It's no stretch to say they accomplished it. Olio e Limone quickly gained a reputation for having the best Italian food in town.

Eighteen years later, the menu isn't stale, and the locals still love it. "The majority of our guests are locals," Elaine Morello told me. "Even during the summer months."

Try their pumpkin ravioli and spaghetti allo scoglio (with fresh Dungeness crab meat) if you have the chance, and don't be shy with the bottle of proprietary olive oil that's on the table. It's delicious!

Olio Pizzeria—Suite #21

A more casual pizza concept, Olio Pizzeria opened in 2010 and hasn't had a slow night since. You never know who you'll see here. Last time I went, Michael Keaton was enjoying a meal at the bar.

This is the one to visit for cocktails, pizza, and a seemingly infinite selection of delectable appetizers. Try the calamari al nero di seppia; the batter is mixed with squid ink, so it's served pitch black with a refreshing lemon aioli. Or tuck into crostini spread with almonds, ricotta, honey, and cherries before moving on to tackle a thin-crust pizza spread with your choice of toppings.

For a better version of your favorite childhood pizza party, call ahead and reserve one of the two private dining rooms.

Type: Italian
Neighborhood: Downtown
Price: $-$$$

Top: The elegant dining room at Olio e Limone has a great view of wine. Photo by Kevin Steele

Above left: This is the place to go for specialty Italian dishes, like this taglioni del campo, with leeks, spinach, green beans, and parmesan. Photo by Kevin Steele

Above right: For thin-crust pizzas and a wide array of Italian appetizers, Olio Pizzeria is a smart choice. Photo by Kevin Steele

Olio Crudo Bar—Suite #18

Olio Crudo looks and is a little fancy, but it also kind of secretly has one of the best happy hours in Santa Barbara. This jewel box of a crudo shop is all windows and shine, and it's a tasty place to visit for barrel-aged cocktails paired with raw seafood, Italian meats, and other small dishes.

The most recent addition to the Olio family, the crudo bar was inspired by the owners' own food needs. "We had most of our favorite dishes offered already between Olio e Limone Ristorante and Olio Pizzeria, but were missing our preferred things to eat late at night when we can finally grab a bite and often feel like just some light crudo," said Morello.

11 West Victoria St.
805-899-2699
oliocucina.com

ON THE ALLEY

Fact: a sunny seaside day in Santa Barbara should include a meal from On The Alley. This casual venue brought to you by the owners of Brophy Bros., Santa Barbara's wildly popular seafood restaurant, serves fresh catches and kid-approved favorites like tater tots and grilled cheeses.

With a lunch and dinner menu full of crisp fish tacos, tasty sandwiches, and burgers, On The Alley sells tasty eats in view of the harbor. Included on the menu are a handful of Brophy Bros. classics like clam chowder, ceviche, and fish and chips. More adventurous eaters should order the crab cake burger or pulled pork sandwich. Most items come with housemade potato or tortilla chips, but you should do yourself a favor and upgrade to fries or tots.

Breakfast is also served, and it can be a real treat because the harbor is a little less busy then. Imagine walking the breakwater, spotting some dolphins, and then getting three eggs scrambled with cheese, avocado, and tater tots served in a hearty breakfast bowl for less than $10. Magical, right? Or digging into a plate of waffle "fries"—waffles cut into strips and deep fried, served with maple syrup for dipping. It's all possible (and all delicious) here.

Place your order at the counter and lay claim to a table outside. Your food will be brought to you when it's ready. Communal seating is available in front of the restaurant, or you can take your food to go. The one catch is that On The Alley closes fairly early, usually around 7 p.m., so you have to remember to go sometime before it gets dark.

As if the sea air, generous portions, and wallet-friendly prices aren't already enough to ensure a feel-good experience, everything in the

Type: Seafood
Neighborhood: Waterfront
Price: $-$$
Try the: Fried Avocado Taco, Fish Taco, Tater Tots
Great for: Al Fresco Dining, Breakfast, Lunch

Top left: Shown here: one fried fish taco and one fried avocado taco.

Top right: Although primarily a seafood restaurant, fish isn't your only option here, as evidenced by this burger and tots.

Above left: On The Alley also serves beer and hard cider.

Above right: Early risers should stop by for breakfast by the harbor. The Ty's muffin is delicious.

restaurant—from the floor tiles to the refrigeration units—is a result of the owners' commitment to using only products that are made in the USA.

And there's even more good news! Another location has recently opened up for our friends in Goleta. It serves a very similar menu. Visit the website for more details.

117 Harbor Way
805-962-6315
onthealley.com

OUTPOST

When you pull up to the Goodland Hotel, which is where Outpost is located, your first thought probably won't be, "Wow, this was definitely a Holiday Inn!" But it was, before the Kimpton brand of boutique hotels stepped in and "presto chango," the property was transformed into something a little hipper, a little more "Palm Springs meets surf culture."

You'll see walls with colorful murals, lacquered surfboards hung from the ceiling, a tiny record shop (with real vinyl), and oodles of macramé. And suddenly you won't feel like you're in Goleta anymore. That feeling will stay with you when you cross the lobby to the restaurant, a unique indoor-outdoor space with graphic floor tiles and a pool view.

Not to be outdone, chef James Siao's menu is full of surprises too, with quirky dishes that you won't find elsewhere in town. Which is what makes it worth the drive from Santa Barbara; even locals like to pop in and see what's going on out here.

This is a place you want to visit for brunch, dinner, or poolside eats. Brunch is pretty indulgent. Think mole burritos, jalapeño fritter Benedicts, and steak and eggs drizzled with chimichurri. Want something lighter? I don't know, does a bacon tart count?

At dinner, your best plan is to share a few small plates. The oysters are always fresh, and the bibimbap with barbecued octopus is great. On second thought, you probably won't want to share that. Outpost has a fun "pick three" menu concept that allows you to try what you like from their taco and bao bun assortment. You can get tacos so

Type: Californian
Neighborhood: Goleta
Price: $$
Try the: Any Empanada, Bibimbap,
Seafood Scrapple Bao Bun
Great for: Happy Hour, Weeknights, Pool Dining

Top left: Start off with some Pacific oysters and a beer.

Above left: Outpost's creative cocktail program matches the enthusiasm of the food.

Right: Poolside brunch is fun on the weekends. Check out these super-fancy chilaquiles.

many places in the area, but the Outpost's soft bao treats are much harder to come by and very tasty.

The restaurant has a good beer and wine menu, but the bar program is particularly impressive. It takes its signature drinks seriously, mixing spirits with fresh ingredients instead of overwhelming them with syrupy flavors. If you like cocktails, you'll find something to love on the Outpost's drink list. And if that list somehow fails you, there's another bar right across the foyer with an equally impressive but altogether different selection.

5650 Calle Real, Goleta
805-964-1288
outpostsb.com

PACIFIC PICKLE WORKS

If you love pickles, you're in luck! Santa Barbara happens to be home to some of the tastiest pickles around. All natural and handcrafted using produce grown in California, you'll find Pacific Pickle Works's briny creations included in menu items and stocked on shelves all over town.

These locally produced and packaged eats offer far more than your standard dills. Bradley Bennett, Principal Pickle at Pacific Pickle Works, pickles everything from asparagus and cauliflower to okra and beets.

Like many successful businesses, this one started at home. "Each fall I would make pickles and hand out the jars as gifts for the holidays," explains Bennett. "The list of people expecting those pickles grew and grew to a point where I decided I either needed to start selling them or retire the holiday pickle production. So here I am with a pickle company!"

Think pickles are just for snacking? Or worse, garnish? Think again. You'll find cocktails and munchies that include Bennett's pickles throughout Santa Barbara. And it's not just professional chefs who are having fun with them.

"We love talking new recipes at Pacific Pickle Works. And so many of them come from ideas our customers bring to us," he said. "I recently had a customer suggest substituting chopped pickled beets for the chopped pickles in a deviled egg recipe. The result is a beautiful pink stuffed deviled egg. We call them Unbeetable Deviled Eggs. Another fun use is a pickled grilled cheese. Try chopping up some pickled Brussels sprouts and asparagus and putting them in a

Type: Pickles
Price: $
Try the: Cukarambas, Jalabeaños, Unbeetables

Left: Behind the scenes jarring Stokra, hot pickled okra.

Right: The Pacific Pickle Works Bloody Mary Basket has all the fixings for everyone's favorite brunch cocktail, seen here with locally distilled Cutler's Vodka.

grilled Gouda and white sharp cheddar cheese sandwich—it's more Gouda!"

Silly food puns aside, they take their business seriously, with pickles available for sale in retailers like Whole Foods throughout California, Arizona, Nevada, and Hawaii, as well as a handful of locations in the greater United States.

Enthusiasts can also join their Pickle Club. It's kind of like a wine club, but with more vinegar and less alcohol. For a flat fee, members receive quarterly shipments of seasonal vegetables. Gherkin members get two jars and Big Dill members get four. Pickles can be shipped anywhere in the US or picked up at Pacific Pickle Works's local factory, where you just might get to say hello to the Principal Pickle himself.

"One of the greatest things about being in Santa Barbara is getting to know such a great community of food and beverage makers and participating in the shared passion that drives them," added Bennett.

805-765-1PPW (1779)
pacificpickleworks.com

PADARO BEACH GRILL

You'd be hard-pressed to find a restaurant with better scenery in Santa Barbara, maybe even California, than Padaro Beach Grill. Overlooking Santa Claus Beach—a sandy local favorite less than ten miles south of downtown—the Padaro Beach Grill boasts a breathtaking outdoor dining room that's ideal for family meals, day dates, and impromptu gatherings.

Enjoy fresh salads, savory burgers, and sinfully rich milkshakes that are made to order and blended by hand. Try the shrimp and avocado salad or dig into a 100 percent USDA lean beef burger paired with a side of sweet potato fries. There are also sandwiches and seafood specialties, and you can ditch the bread or bun in favor of a lettuce wrap. The menu takes great care to let you know that the kitchen uses non-GMO produce and trans-fat-free oil in its fryers. Padaro's broad but uncomplicated offerings make it an easy place to go with almost anyone.

You place your order at the inside counter, then enjoy your meal outside. The outdoor dining space resembles a park. Lush green grass is dotted with picnic tables, some with shade, some in full sun. There is plenty of room for little ones to run around. An epic sandbox encourages the kiddos to play while grownups indulge in refreshing beers and local wines.

Padaro Beach Grill is open every day, from just before lunch until 8 p.m. Live bands are common on the weekends, giving the place a beach party atmosphere. You can throw your own party here if you want to, in fact. Padaro is a good choice for rehearsal dinners, birthday parties, and corporate events.

Type: Californian
Neighborhood: Carpinteria
Price: $$
Try the: Pretzel Burger, Shrimp & Avocado Salad, Milkshakes
Great for: Kids, Families, Lunch

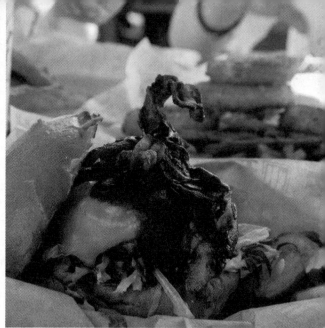

Top left: Padaro Beach Grill fronts Santa Claus Beach.

Above left: A giant sandbox keeps the kiddos busy.

Above right: Dig into bacon burgers and onion rings under the summer sun.

There's free (but often crowded) parking right out front. If you get stressed about parallel parking when herds of people in swim trunks are milling about, you might want to let someone else drive. The good news is that you just have to park once to enjoy an awesome beach day made even better by stellar eats, so that's a win by any measure!

3766 Santa Claus Lane, Carpinteria
805-566-9800
padarobeachgrill.com

THE PALACE GRILL

The Palace opened in Santa Barbara in 1985 and deserves to be included in this book, but I have to be upfront and tell you that this entry is exceptionally biased. I met my husband at The Palace. During college I worked at the bikini shop next door, and he was the charming waiter who would always pop by with extra soufflés from the kitchen (it turns out they weren't really "extra"). And the rest, as they say, is history. In fact, if you use the restroom on the left side of the building, there is a painting of the aqua beach cruiser I rode to work every day in the tile work above the sink.

Bias and handsome wait staff notwithstanding, The Palace is a fun local Cajun restaurant with a New Orleans vibe that deserves a visit. The interior is decked out with paintings of musicians, Mardi Gras beads, and boxes of beignet mix. You will have the best time if you go with at least one other person and you're feeling festive. Birthdays, anniversaries, life…it doesn't really matter what you're celebrating—when you're at The Palace, it's time to do as the menu suggests and "laissez les bon temps rouler!"

The Palace serves lunch and dinner seven days a week. Whatever you're in the mood for, it's a good idea to start with a beverage. The Cajun martini is legendary—jalapeño-infused vodka garnished with cherry peppers and served by the pint or quart. What's next? A basket of freshly baked muffins will show up at your table while you review your options.

"The most popular menu items have to be the crawfish popcorn and redfish," said Errol Williams, the general manager who has been at the restaurant for twenty-four years. "But I love the rack of lamb

Type: Cajun
Neighborhood: Downtown
Price: $$–$$$
Try the: Soft-Shell Crab, Blackened Redfish, Cajun Martini
Great for: Dates, Celebrations, Anniversaries

Welcome to The Palace!

- Please take a place behind the last person in line

- There is no need to give your name, as guests are seated in the order they arrive

- The host will be out momentarily to confirm the number in your party

Thank you

Top right: Load up on Cajun favorites at The Palace Grill—you won't come away hungry!

Above left: General Manager Errol Williams keeping the Friday night line in check.

Above right: This restaurant is known for its soufflés, but the under-the-radar dessert favorite is definitely the key lime pie.

and soft-shell crab. Don't be afraid to be adventurous. Try new items; you just might be surprised!" I recommend trying the Oysters Palace, pan BBQ shrimp, and jambalaya.

There are two things to keep in mind when you're planning a visit. First, The Palace doesn't take reservations. Well, it does, but only at 5:30 p.m. After that, prepare for a wait in a small line, often with a live band or magician there to keep your mind off your hunger. Second, The Palace has won dozens of awards for best service. The staff here works as a team, meaning anyone may be your server at any moment. This is especially fun on rowdy nights when they come by your table singing and clinking glasses.

8 East Cota St.
805-963-5000
palacegrill.com

THE PALMS

I'm not sure if anything is more distinctive than going to a one-hundred-plus-year-old restaurant where you cook your own steak, chicken, fish, and more. But that's just what you'll find at The Palms, a steakhouse that's been a Carpinteria tradition since 1912.

The Palms is located right in the heart of downtown; in fact, it feels like the town sprang up around it. It was built as a hotel at the turn of the century and was pretty much the only place you could get a beer in the area. Now this two-story building is home to one of the few full bars in Carp, making it a lively meeting spot for generations of locals.

The Palms's menu is printed on their placemats and offers hearty appetizers—including crab cocktail, hot wings, and jalapeño poppers—and even heartier main courses of the surf or turf variety. Think Alaskan king crab, filet mignon, and full racks of lamb. All dinners include a trip to the salad bar as well as bread, baked beans, and a foil-wrapped baked potato. For the most part, prices are shockingly reasonable. Vegetarians can take a trip to the salad bar and get all the sides for less than $10.

You can absolutely get food that's expertly cooked for you here, but it's probably more fun to do it yourself on one of the two lava rock gas grills in the center of the restaurant. These were added in 1968 by then-owner Kenneth Anderson and have been a popular attraction ever since. Your item will be delivered to you raw—then you just sidle on up and get to sizzling. If your meat ends up over- or underdone, it's your own fault!

Type: Steakhouse
Neighborhood: Carpinteria
Price: $$
Try the: Hot Wings, Rib Eye, Filet Mignon
Great for: Drinks, Special Occasions, Reunions

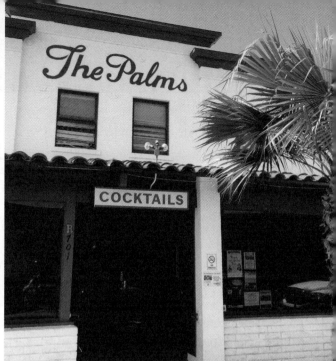

Top left: You cook your meat yourself at The Palms. Sure, there are a few things they cook for you, but that's not as much fun.

Above left: Inside has sort of a saloon-like feeling, drawing crowds for stiff drinks every night.

Above right: The outside of The Palms doesn't look all that different than it did when it first opened in 1912.

To round out the already killer food-and-booze combo, The Palms is home to live music several nights a week. Check out the not-always-updated entertainment calendar on the website to see what might be coming up.

Like I said earlier, this restaurant and bar is centrally located, so it's not a good place to go if you're hoping to enjoy a quiet meal and keep a low profile. If, however, you're looking to make new friends or run into some old ones, The Palms is an excellent choice.

701 Linden Ave., Carpinteria
805-684-3811
thepalmscarpinteria.com

PARADISE CAFE

The Paradise Cafe has been open since 1983. That might seem like a long time, but to hear locals tell it, it's been a part of Santa Barbara since…I don't know, food was invented? Everyone who lives here has been in for a burger at least once. If they tell you otherwise, they are lying.

Perched on a prime corner just one block off State Street, the Paradise is the definition of "charming" at first sight. The sugar-white building and surrounding garden space are home to a dining room, a bar, and a killer patio.

The menu here is full of California classics. You'll see steaks, swordfish, eggplant, and artichokes. But the thing that makes the food a standout is that it's fired over an oak-wood grill. The Paradise has the first and only grill within city limits that uses Santa Maria live oak to do the bulk of their cooking.

Although everything here is pretty tasty, the Paradise—as mentioned above—is perhaps best known for its burgers. Served hot, at a reasonable price, with optional cheese and grilled onions, these burgers can fix almost anything—hangovers, bad days, hurt feelings. Piled high with skinny fries and drenched with Paradise sauce (essentially, chunky Thousand Island), the Paradise burger is a cure. Turkey and veggie patties are available too, meaning everyone can get in on the fun.

Because there are lots of not-too-exotic options, it's a solid choice for a family or work dinner. The wide, sunny patio is raised off the street, giving you a great view of passing downtown traffic. The bar is well provisioned and has plenty of room for people without

Type: American
Neighborhood: Downtown
Price: $$
Try the: Burgers, Kebabs, Paradise Pie
Great for: Brunch, Lunch, Patio Dining, Happy Hour

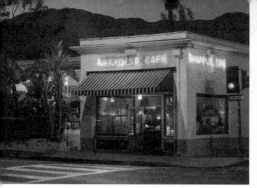

Left: The Paradise Cafe is a corner restaurant with a beautiful open-air patio. Photo by Chuck Place Photography

Right: The grilled artichoke is loaded with fresh salsa.

reservations. It's also an extremely comfortable place to grab brunch and a bloody mary, maybe while you catch a game on TV. I hear the Paradise has great eggs; I've just never been able to order eggs knowing I could order a burger instead.

Probably the best thing about the Paradise, though, is just what a part of the fabric of Santa Barbara it is. The mural facing the patio depicts old-time movie star and Santa Barbara Fiesta favorite Leo Carrillo on horseback. Legend has it that this was one of Carrillo's favorite haunts after the Fiesta parade, and he was known to tie up his horse in front of the restaurant during his annual visit. Whether true or not, it's still a Santa Barbara institution during Fiesta. I know of at least two unofficial parade groups that stop by here for margaritas and snacks after watching the pretty ponies pass by.

702 Anacapa St.
805-962-4416
paradisecafe.com

THE PICKLE ROOM

It's hard to write about The Pickle Room. A few years back, a short film called *Grasshoppers for Grandpa* came out that charted the history of this place, and that movie tells the story of this legendary establishment better than I ever could.

The Pickle Room didn't start out as The Pickle Room. The building is one of the few remaining relics of Santa Barbara's Chinatown area. Before this, it was a local landmark called Jimmy's Oriental Gardens, a Chinese bar and restaurant run by the Chung family since 1947.

Jimmy's was passed from father to son and was known for a friendly atmosphere and great mai tais until it closed somewhat suddenly in 2006, much to the dismay of its regulars.

The building—deemed a historic site—sat unoccupied for a few years while the town debated what to do with it. A sandwich shop expanded into one side of the building, while the other side remained closed. Rumor had it that it might become a museum, much to the disappointment of locals who had been whetting their whistles at Jimmy's for decades.

Then, in 2013, there was a wonderful turn of events. With seemingly little notice, the place reopened to thirsty patrons everywhere. What happened? The owners of Three Pickles, the deli next door, took over, renaming it The Pickle Room, although the old Jimmy's sign hangs behind the bar inside.

Thanks to the care of the Lovejoys, who were Jimmy's customers before taking ownership, walking into The Pickle Room today isn't

Type: Chinese/American
Neighborhood: Downtown
Price: $-$$
Try the: Fried Rice, Smitty Burger, Mai Tai
Great for: Happy Hour, History Buffs

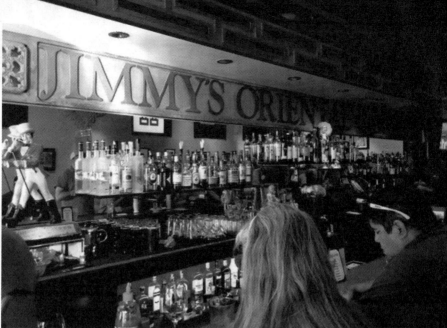

Top left: Head to The Pickle Room for powerful drinks and flavorful eats in a historic building that's a remnant from Santa Barbara's Chinatown.

Left center: Get the Smitty burger—bigger than a slider but smaller than your typical burger, these beefy dreams are a deal during happy hour. Photo by Aron Ives

Above left: If you're here, you might as well have a classic mai tai.

Above right: The original Jimmy's Oriental Gardens sign still hangs behind the bar.

all that different from walking into Jimmy's decades ago. You'll probably even see some of the same people gathered around the long bar.

It's a seamless combination of old and new Santa Barbara. You can still drink mai tais just like Willy used to make. Exactly the same actually, if you pop in on a night he's bartending. Until recently, it was as close to a tiki bar as the town had, so there are also Singapore slings and other fun cocktails served in tropical glassware.

The small but delicious food menu combines deli staples with traditional Chinese dishes in an oddly satisfying way. Try Reuben eggrolls and panko fried pickles. The fried rice is served with an egg with a Sriracha smiley face on top, and the Smitty burgers are definitely worth ordering in multiple. (They're small, so it's okay.)

126 East Canon Perdido St.

805-965-1015

PRESIDIO MARKET

When I asked my husband which type of food I should call the meals sold at Presidio Market, he said "late-night stoner food." I don't know if that will fly with my publishers, but we're giving it a shot. Because he's not wrong.

To our credit (or detriment), I haven't been there late at night. Maybe it's because I'm too lazy. Maybe it's because my night vision isn't the type you want driving a car without a full moon. Whatever the case, I can assure you that the menu items here hold up at all hours of the day.

It doesn't hurt that everything costs less than $10. And it's also not a bummer that you can get a burrito, a club sandwich, and falafels all at once.

But probably the best thing about this restaurant—the most refreshing "I know something you don't know" thing—is that it's not a restaurant at all. Go ahead. Google Earth it. It's a liquor store.

When you get there, you'll have to pass by the aisles of chips and beer and fancy hard alcohol marketing displays until you get to the very back. There, you'll find a small window with a menu above it and utensils lining the opening. This is where you'll get some of the best late-night eats in town. You're welcome.

1236 Santa Barbara St.
805-965-8770
presidiomarketanddeli.com

Left: This pretty normal-looking convenience store is your secret gateway to late-night eats.

Right: You've got to walk all the way back to place your order at this tiny window.

Type: International
Neighborhood: Downtown
Price: $
Try the: Breakfast Burrito, Falafel Plate
Great for: Late Night, Early Morning, Takeout

RENAUD'S PATISSERIE & BISTRO

Through some grievous oversight, Renaud's Patisserie & Bistro almost wasn't included in this book. I don't understand how that happened because I have literally spent hours extolling the virtues of Renaud's croissants. If you like pastries—and I don't, particularly—you'll love this bakery. If you don't, well, apparently you'll love it anyway.

The fact of the matter is, the best chocolate croissant you will ever enjoy is not waiting for you in Paris. (Sorry if that shakes up some plans for intercontinental travel, but don't worry, they still have the best escargot.) No, it is right here in Santa Barbara, waiting, nay, beckoning from the beautiful glass case at Renaud's.

Before you even take the first bite, you know there is something different about this croissant, something that makes it superior to any previous croissant you've eaten. Just put one finger on the shell, and you will feel the difference. The crust is so flaky and perfectly baked that it literally shatters at the touch! And yet somehow, through a magical method likely known only to Monsieur Renaud, the interior is still moist and chewy. And the chocolate? Of the highest quality, dark yet sweet and not too much. The almond croissants aren't shabby, either, mounded with glazed almond slices and not overfilled with almond paste.

The offerings at this French-style bakery go far beyond croissants too. Renaud Gonthier, co-founder and executive pastry chef, brings his extensive experience as a top pastry chef at venues around the world to his bistro on upper State Street. It serves an extensive breakfast and

Type: Bakery
Neighborhood: Upper State
Price: $-$$
Try the: Chocolate Croissant, Almond Croissant, Macarons
Great for: Coffee, Breakfast, Treating Yourself

Top: Renaud's Patisserie & Bistro is definitely not gluten-free.

Above left: The almond croissant is ridiculously decadent.

Above right: I would put chef Renaud Gonthier's chocolate croissant up against any you find in Paris.

lunch menu inspired by the Provence region of France and Gonthier's personal favorites.

Breakfast includes toasted homemade baguettes and brioches, served with butter and homemade jam, as well as more substantial egg dishes. For lunch, you might indulge in a croque monsieur or sate yourself with a ratatouille tartine.

But the real draw here, besides the sun-filled front patio, is the pastry case, full to bursting with not just croissants but tarts, eclairs, and macarons of every flavor and color.

Everyone here loves Renaud's, so there is now another location downtown that is just as charming, if not more so, but has a smaller selection. Renaud's also supplies some of the grocers and coffee shops in town with baguettes and other baked goods.

3315 State St.
805-569-2400
renaudsbakery.com

ROSE CAFÉ

There are two Rose Café locations for now, and they both have their merits, but this entry is for the one on the Mesa. It stands out because it is a restaurant with a very tropical-feeling patio—the kind of place where you want to meet your friends for brunch—and because there is some remarkably valuable art on the walls. The menu is affordable and delicious and you could treat your parents to dinner here without going broke. And they have some of the best ice in town. Okay, convinced yet? No? I can go on.

Opened seventy years ago, the Rose Café is a family business. This location is one of the few sit-down, full-service Mexican restaurants in town. Certainly, affordable sit-down service Mexican restaurants are in the minority in Santa Barbara. Usually you're waiting in line at a taco joint or ordering at a counter, then waiting for your number. Otherwise you're enjoying some sort of linens and delicate mole sauce situation, and that's fine too. But here you can sit, take your time, and chow down on some traditional dishes while being served in a leisurely fashion.

All the classics are present and accounted for on the menu. There are tostadas, red and green enchiladas, chiles rellenos, and plates of lengua simmered in tomatillo salsa. Chips are served fresh and warm before your entrée. And that ice I mentioned? It's the nugget kind you might remember from roller rinks or other such nostalgic places, the kind that makes sodas seem even more carbonated. If you're thirsty for something stronger, they have great blended margaritas—the strawberry ones aren't artificially dyed red—and a nice list of beer and tequila.

Type: Mexican
Neighborhood: Mesa
Price: $-$$
Try the: Chilaquiles, Chorizo Enchiladas, Strawberry Margaritas
Great for: Brunch, Family Meals, Celebrations

Left: Chilaquiles at Rose Café can be made to suit your preferred spice level.

Right: The colorful patio feels like vacation, and inside is just as vibrant.

Lunch and dinner are both reliably delicious, but breakfast is incredible. Once you've had the chilaquiles here, you will spend the rest of your life comparing every other version unfavorably to this dish.

And the art? This warm, colorful restaurant is hung with original paintings by Dan Lutz, a very famous midcentury California painter. (Usually his work hangs in museums like LACMA.)

One word of caution: this restaurant closes for an extended family vacation during the last two weeks of the year. Inevitably, you'll crave Rose Café's warm, home-cooked Mexican food at exactly this time and drive there, only to be disappointed. It's happened to me; don't say I didn't warn you!

1816 Cliff Dr.
805-965-5513
rosecafe2.com

RUSTY'S PIZZA

In this age of smartphones, a lot of us don't have phone numbers memorized anymore. If you lost your phone, I bet you could call your parents, your significant other, and maybe your best friend. And if you live in Santa Barbara, you could probably call and order a pizza.

There are eight Rusty's Pizzas in the area—and oddly, nine in Bakersfield—and they all use the same phone number. I'm not going to try to tell you that Rusty's is the best pizza in Santa Barbara; on most nights it probably isn't, but it's the most consistent pizza by leaps and bounds. And it delivers. In this town with limited food delivery services, that counts for a lot.

Rusty's got its start in Isla Vista, the college neighborhood surrounding UCSB, way back in 1969. Although it has expanded rapidly since then, it still remains rooted in the community, sponsoring numerous school programs and youth organizations. And it's still got the same phone number.

The pizza here is dependably good. You don't get an overdone pizza one time and an underdone pie the next. They're never not open when they say they will be—a common problem with other pizza delivery places in the area. You can choose from thin or thick pan crust and about twenty toppings. There are five specialty pizzas on the menu as well as hot wings, subs, salads, and garlic bread. Delivery is free, and there are pretty much always coupons arriving in the mail and hanging out on counters at local hotels.

Type: Pizza
Neighborhood: All
Price: $
Try the: Pizza (duh)
Great for: Delivery, Parties, Families, Students

Top left: This cheesy goodness is a familiar sight for any local.

Above left: Get a behind-the-scenes tour with the Rusty's team if you call ahead.

Above right: The downtown Rusty's location is easy to spot, and there are fun games upstairs.

Don't want to call the most memorized number ever? No big deal, you can also order online. Hot, fresh, local pizza is literally just a few clicks away.

Although it's most convenient to get your order delivered, a visit to Rusty's can be pretty fun. Most locations have big screen TVs and video or arcade games. There are private rooms you can reserve for a party. If you call ahead, Rusty's managers can even arrange a tour for your group. Go see the pizza-making process and make your own (individual) pizza to enjoy after the tour!

Multiple locations
Santa Barbara, Carpinteria, and Goleta
805-564-1111
rustyspizza.com

SAMA SAMA KITCHEN

When Sama Sama Kitchen first opened in 2013, its Indonesian-inspired menu was a refreshing addition to the Santa Barbara food scene. Many of us were ready for soft bao buns, savory noodles, and peanutty tempeh tacos, but was the town? In a land of Mediterranean everything, it seemed like an iffy bet for chef Ryan Simorangkir and Shelter Social Club, part of the creative team behind the restaurant.

Thankfully, their efforts to pair the lively flavors of Southeast Asia with fresh ingredients from local markets have paid off. Sama Sama is more than a restaurant; it's a part of the community.

Open for dinner seven nights a week, Sama Sama usually offers a happy hour menu during the week and a late-night menu on the weekends. Availability changes with the seasons, but there are a few classics you will always be able to order. Start with an order of crispy krupuk and sambal while you survey your options, then plan on ordering multiple dishes to share.

The chicken wings here are sticky and delicious, glazed with a sweet soy tamarind sauce and a fresh squeeze of lime. If you like noodles, try the nasi goreng and get a warm pile of chewy noodles topped with soft scrambled eggs, Asian greens, and shrimp crackers. Large plates vary more frequently, but as I write there's a really hearty roasted Kurobuta pork belly on there, paired with black pepper-leek rice porridge, organic sunny side up egg, soy, sesame oil, and garlic crackers.

The restaurant looks deceptively small at first glance. Narrow and fronted with a bar—that has wonderful cocktails, by the way—it runs out to the back to a patio with a secret garden feel. Decked with

Type: Indonesian
Neighborhood: Downtown
Price: $$
Try the: Cocktails, Jidori Wings, Nasi Goreng
Great for: Dates, Drinks, Gatherings

Top right: Visit the cozy back patio that is worlds away from the bustle of State Street. Photo by Cara Robbins

Above left: Sama Sama is a restaurant built for sharing. Photo by Cara Robbins

Above right: Don't miss the unusual cocktail menu when you go in for a meal. Photo by Cara Robbins

handsomely hewn communal tables, fresh herb and veggie gardens, and romantic twinkling lights, this is where you want to sit on warm summer nights. You'll be right in the center of downtown with a view of the stars.

This is also where all the fun happens. As mentioned earlier, Sama Sama takes an active role in the Santa Barbara food and culture scene. They support other local businesses by hosting launch parties, art shows, pop-up dinners, collaborations, and more, with most activities happening out back.

If you're looking for someplace to have a memorable meal and get a taste of what's going on locally, this is it.

1208 State St.
805-965-4566
samasamakitchen.com

SANTA BARBARA CERTIFIED FARMERS MARKET

One of the most magical things about Santa Barbara, particularly for food enthusiasts, is that there's a farmers' market happening somewhere in town six days a week. With the exception of Monday, you can head out with just a few bucks and some reusable bags and come back with a local bounty of flavors that are fresh off the farm.

From fruits and vegetables to meats and cheeses, the makings for any good meal or picnic start here. Seafood vendors also make an appearance, and you'll often find something you hadn't anticipated, like whole rabbits or freshly pulled milk. The association of more than one hundred purveyors, owned and operated by the members and its board of directors, is committed to helping promote local family farmers and protecting the surrounding environment.

There are markets downtown as well as in Goleta, Carpinteria, Montecito, and Solvang. Each of the markets has its own personality, but every one of them is fun. There's nothing intimidating about them. You don't have to be a chef or nutritionist to enjoy a stroll through the stalls.

My favorite market is the Tuesday night one because it's right in the middle of downtown. The city closes off State Street from Ortega to Haley so shoppers can wander freely. You can buy flowers, herbs, and pasta, listen to buskers playing live music, and then pop into a nearby shop or duck into a bar to enjoy happy hour.

Type: Market
Price: $-$$
Try the: Cheese and Produce Samples, Local Eggs,
Hope Ranch Mussels

Top right: Traveling? Take home some non-perishables like these award-winning jams.

Above left: Gorgeous strawberries are available almost year-round.

Above right: Get produce straight from the source at one of Santa Barbara's seven weekly farmers' markets.

The farmers' market website has an updated schedule as well as a helpful list of what's in season, so you can search alphabetically for almost anything you're hoping to find. The website also features a changing selection of recipes in case you're stumped for what to make or just looking for something new to try.

Even if you're only in town for a few days and don't have access to a full kitchen, the farmers' market is still worth a visit. Besides being a beautiful place to take photos and learn more about local agriculture, there are plenty of shelf-stable souvenirs you can take home with you. Grab a bunch of fragrant dried lavender or pick up a jar of gold medal award-winning tangelo and kumquat marmalade. Both will serve as sunny reminders of your trip, and neither will spoil on the return journey.

sbfarmersmarket.org

SANTA BARBARA FISHERMAN'S MARKET

Attention seafood enthusiasts: prepare to work up an appetite and set your alarm clocks! If you're in Santa Barbara, the Santa Barbara Fisherman's Market is your can't-miss destination on Saturday mornings.

You have to wake up early to get the freshest catches at this weekly dockside meetup of local fishermen; it's like a farmers' market for fish at the Santa Barbara Harbor. From roughly 7:30 a.m. to noon every Saturday (weather permitting), area fishing crews set up tables and sell their most recent catches, either recently killed or still alive.

Catches range from scaly to spiky to spiny at the Fisherman's Market, depending on the time of year. You can usually find lingcod and rockfish. Seasonal specialties include spiny lobster and giant Santa Barbara spot prawns. They're at least twice the size of the largest prawn you've ever eaten. Sometimes you find killer deals, like crab for $5 a pound.

And then, if you're really, really early, you might luck onto a pile of Santa Barbara sea urchin. These spiky purple sea creatures are prized for their delicious interior morsels. It's called uni, and it pops up on the fanciest menus around the world. Santa Barbara has some of the most famous urchin, much of which is shipped off to Japan and other countries. But here at the market, you can buy a live urchin for less than $10, crack it open, and eat it on the spot.

Type: Seafood
Neighborhood: Waterfront
Price: $-$$
Try the: Crabs, Uni, Santa Barbara Spot Prawns
Great for: Seafood Lovers, Early Birds

Top left: Early bird catches the crab! Inexpensive by the pound, these beauties sell out quickly.

Above left: Shop for seafood directly from local fishermen.

Above right: Nothing to see here . . . just a tub of giant live lobsters.

Photos courtesy of Commercial Fishermen of Santa Barbara.

Late risers who miss the Fisherman's Market but still have a hankering for some halibut can head to the similarly named Santa Barbara Fish Market, also located in the harbor area. The Santa Barbara Fish Market is open seven days a week and sells locally caught fish and shellfish from its small, unassuming storefront. It offers everything from raw tuna and smoked salmon to oysters and seaweed salad.

Keep in mind that both the Santa Barbara Fisherman's Market and the Santa Barbara Fish Market are seafood purveyors, not restaurants (although the Fish Market will shuck oysters and crack uni for you if they have the time).

Navy Pier
805-654-5531
cfsb.info

SANTA BARBARA POPCORN COMPANY

You might occasionally find yourself hungry in between mealtimes. In these instances, it's a good idea to reach for a snack. Fortunately, Santa Barbara produces a number of great snacks, like avocados. For something crunchier, how about some popcorn?

Santa Barbara Popcorn Company bags up a delicious snack food made with high-quality ingredients. And you don't even need utensils to eat it! It's the perfect grab-and-go hunger solution for a picnic, trip to the beach, or hike.

"Our butterfly kernels are grown by the only certified organic popcorn farmer in California," said Christopher Pollastrini, chief kernel in charge (full disclosure: I made that title up). "Farmer Ed Sills and his family run Pleasant Grove Farms, a second-generation family-owned farm."

Christopher and his helpers take a great base ingredient and make it even better by popping it right here in town and adding inventive seasonings. There are a number of flavors available at any given point, but Sea Salt & Olive Oil is the perpetual best seller. The resulting product is a fresh bag of popcorn that's GMO- and gluten-free, vegan, whole grain, and California grown and contains neither artificial ingredients nor trans fat.

Santa Barbara Popcorn Company popcorn is available at dozens of locations around town, including stores, hotels, and wine-tasting rooms.

805-628-2177
sbpopcorn.com

Left: Sea Salt & Olive Oil is a light and crisp treat, made from certified organic corn.

Right: While Santa Barbara Popcorn makes a variety of flavors, Balsamic Vinegar & Italian Herb is the best seller.

Type: Popcorn
Price: $
Try the: Balsamic Vinegar & Italian Herbs,
Maple & Brown Sugar

SANTA BARBARA SHELLFISH COMPANY

You might not believe this, but there's a real gem of a restaurant in the middle of a bunch of tourist traps on the wharf. That's right, way down at the very end of the pier, there's a seafood restaurant worth every penny of the menu prices. Possibly more. (Let's hope they don't read this.)

Seafood doesn't get any fresher than it does here. At the Santa Barbara Shellfish Company, you can pick your lunch right out of the tanks that line the front window. Established in 1980, this restaurant began as a shellfish shop before popular demand—and secret family recipes—transformed it into the bustling eatery it is today.

The first thing you'll notice when you walk up is that it's pretty much a shack. The eaves are lined with dangling buoys, and a sign that reads "Eat Lotsa Lobster" hangs along the roofline. On days that are busy, and most are, you sign your name onto the clipboard outside and wait to be called to sit down.

Inside there are no tables, but there is a bar counter lined with stools that faces the kitchen. The windows that face the Santa Barbara harbor are also lined with counter dining. Outside there are some booths that seat parties of four or so, but everything operates on a first come, first served basis.

The menu here includes all types of shellfish, but live abalones, crabs, and lobsters are the real stars. Many are locally sourced and most are seasonal, so the specials are likely to change from visit to visit. You'll get a whole steamed crab or lobster paired with onion rings and

Type: Seafood
Neighborhood: Waterfront
Price: $$
Try the: Cioppino, Lobster Tacos, Abalone, Local Crab
Great for: Lunch, Early Dinner, Al Fresco Meals

Top left: There's only counter seating in this seaside shellfish shack.

Top right: Peel-and-eat shrimp are messy but worth the effort.

Above left: Get a whole Dungeness crab topped with crispy onion rings.

Above right: Freshly caught lobsters are grilled while you watch.

coleslaw for much less than you'd pay elsewhere. The year-round dishes are great too. The cioppino comes with a crab claw sticking out of it, and all of the tacos are more or less perfect. If you're a fan of clam chowder, there's probably no better place to have some.

Local and domestic beers are available on draft. They pair nicely with a bread bowl of chowder and a hot order of calamari on a cold or foggy day.

In a rush? Then this might not be the place to go. The wait time can get crazy during weekend summers. But there is a workaround. If you're fine with enjoying a more al fresco meal, you can walk around to the left side of the building and order from the takeout window. Not everything is available, but many of the most popular dishes are. Skip the restaurant wait time and take your order to one of the picnic benches on the pier and enjoy the best view in town.

230 Stearns Wharf
805-966-6676
shellfishco.com

SCARLETT BEGONIA

The Scarlett Begonia is really like two businesses in one. There's the Scarlett Begonia proper, the popular brunch spot that also serves lunch and dinner. And then there's Deux Bakery, an offshoot in the same building that bakes all the delicious pastries sold here.

Scarlett Begonia is exactly the sort of place you'd miss if you were walking along State Street. Its pet-friendly patio and warm restaurant are right there—you don't even have to cross the street to get to it—but it's hidden from view all the same.

Everything Scarlett Begonia serves is made in house. From Deux's pastries to ketchup to pickles, it's all whipped up just steps away in the bright and bustling kitchen. The menu includes every dish you want for breakfast—eggs, potatoes, pancakes—made even more delicious. Think scrambles topped with aged Gouda and lemon ricotta pancakes spread with fresh berry compote. And of course there are tasty things you didn't even know you were hungry for to add to the overwhelming choices you have to make when it's time to order. Shrimp and grits with chorizo sausage? Yes, please!

Add to that indulgent beverages, like housemade orange clove soda, Green Star Coffee cappuccinos, and hot chocolate with a campfire marshmallow, and you've just had a meal you'll brag about all day long. They have a full liquor license too, so if you're into day drinking, this is the spot to start. Sip a Liquid Breakfast (maple rye whiskey, organic orange juice, crispy bacon) or refresh yourself with a Toasted Coconut Breeze (aged white rum, coconut simple syrup, limeade, coconut milk float).

Type: Californian
Neighborhood: Downtown
Price: $$
Try the: Toasted Coconut Breeze, Shrimp & Grits, Cinnamon Roll
Great for: Brunch Cocktails, Patio Lunches, Dogs

Top right: Everything at Scarlett Begonia is made from scratch—from the bread to the pickles to the soda.

Above left: Dinner service is attentive, with a focus on Santa Barbara area ingredients.

Above right: Thinking of popping by for weekend brunch? You should definitely make reservations in advance.

Lunch offers a small but carefully curated selection of sandwiches and salads. Dinner has more of a protein focus, ranging from duck confit to pork shank. And happy hour happens Tuesday through Saturday from 4:30 to 6 p.m.

A list of the farms the kitchen sources from is printed on the dinner menus, demonstrating its commitment to local, sustainable, and organic ingredients. It's an extra-special Santa Barbara touch to remind you that this restaurant wouldn't be the same anywhere else.

11 West Victoria St. #10
805-770-2143
scarlettbegonia.net

SEA STEPHANIE FISH

Stephanie Mutz is a person you want to be friends with. She is not only a fisherman and scientist, but also a true food enthusiast with a great sense of humor. If you're looking for someone you can share recipes with and get restaurant recommendations from, you've found her.

But the real reason so many people know her—the reason she's in this book—is her urchin diving. Mutz and her equally cool business partner, Harry Liquornik, dredge up spiny, purple echinoderms from the bottom of the ocean for us to eat. And we're so thankful they do!

"I've been diving since I was seventeen or eighteen. I was a marine biologist, but I got laid off for a bit and started doing deckhand work," said Mutz. "After three years, I entered the lottery for an uni diving license and won. Now I've been an urchin diver for seven years, and I'm teaching science again too."

If you've never had urchin before, here are the basics. The part you eat is called uni. It is golden and creamy and tastes like ocean butter. It is technically the animal's gonads, so you have to crack open the urchin to harvest it. You might see uni perched on top of rice at sushi restaurants or emulsified into a pasta sauce at fine dining Italian restaurants, but uni is at its most delicious when it's fresh out of the shell.

Our local uni is considered some of the best in the world, and a lot of it is shipped elsewhere, including Asia, where it is marked up as a delicacy. But lucky you, here in Santa Barbara you can get fresh urchin for a steal if you buy it directly from the fisherman.

That's where Stephanie comes in. The phone number given is her personal number, and you can call or text her when you're ready to dig into some uni. She and Harry also sell live urchin at various markets, including the Santa Barbara Fisherman's Market

Type: Seafood
Price: $

170

Top right: Urchin diver Stephanie Mutz is a Santa Barbara local you need to know. Photo by Fran Collin

Above left: Find Steph and Harry's fresh catches at area markets. Seen here at the Jolly Oyster tent at Smorgasburg LA.

Above right: Uni tastes best dockside, right out of the shell.

and Smorgasburg LA. Stephanie and Harry rent their boat (and themselves) out for small private parties. If you're feeling extra adventurous, you can arrange to have an intimate uni tasting at the Santa Barbara Harbor.

"My favorite way to eat uni is raw, right on the boat," she shared. "But it's also really good on top of an oyster or smoked with an egg inside."

805-708-4969
seastephaniefish.com

SHINTORI SUSHI FACTORY

First things first—this isn't really a factory. Instead, it's a super-tiny sushi restaurant snuggled into a strip mall on upper State Street.

It's also the first place I ever ate in Santa Barbara, thanks to some misguided soul who directed us here when my parents—who were dropping me off for college—asked for a good place to get chicken. I'm 99 percent sure they weren't asking about teriyaki chicken, but they were good sports about it.

Almost twenty years later, I still don't know much about the chicken here; I've never had it. But the sushi is good, and that's why you should go. Shintori strikes a fine balance between a fancy sushi restaurant and a casual one. The fish is fresh, and the menu has some nice dishes you won't find elsewhere.

The restaurant itself is quite cozy, with one long sushi bar, four tables that seat four, and a counter along the window. There are brightly colored signs and paper lanterns that hang above the seats. You're invited to autograph them while you wait for your food.

The menu is long but not overly so, including starters, classic sushi, house specialties, and donburi bowls. Lunch is offered on weekdays, and dinner is served all week. Free edamame is usually handed out at night too. They have the expected selection of sushi house beers and a decent assortment of filtered and unfiltered sakes.

Type: Japanese
Neighborhood: Upper State
Price: $$
Try the: Shintori Dome, Sunrise Sushi, Pepper Tuna
Great for: Weekday Lunch, Dinner, Groups of Four or Less

Left: Shintori's small dining room is usually full to capacity.

Center: Sit at the bar for the best view of the sushi chefs at work.

Right: Try the Sunrise Sushi, rice wrapped with tuna and topped with raw quail eggs and masago.

Order the famous Shintori Dome and receive a mound of shrimp, raw tuna, salmon, and creamy avocado over a bed of sushi rice. Or try the Sunrise Sushi and get two circles of rice surrounded by thick cuts of fresh tuna, topped with a raw quail egg, and heaped with masago. Popular rolls include the Tie Dye Roll and Gume Roll.

After your meal, you might get some green tea ice cream gratis, but you should really try the Japanese donuts if you've saved any room. They're hot little donut holes covered in sugar with syrup for dipping. And if that isn't sweet enough, fresh fruit and Hershey's Kisses often come with your check.

There's a wait for seats on weekends and service may be slow at peak hours, but the staff really does try to make your stay enjoyable. Due to the shoebox-sized interior, large parties would be best advised to try going elsewhere. But pretty much everyone else should visit Shintori for a light and creative meal in a fun atmosphere.

3001 State St.
805-898-0177
shintorisushi.blogspot.in

THE SHOP
AMERICAN KITCHEN

Want to know where the kids are eating these days? This is it. I know, that sounds like an old person thing to say. I'm only thirty-five, and I always feel like the most ancient person here.

That doesn't stop me from going, though. Because the food is delicious.

If you want brunch without the fuss, this should be high on your list. The Shop makes everything in house, from their bread to their sausages. They serve from 8 a.m. to 3 p.m. every day, and the menu includes cheekily named items like the Rollex (a breakfast wrap in an Indian-style chapatti), Mac on Crack (macaroni and cheese topped with bleu cheese, pecans, and apples), and the YOLO (biscuits and gravy with fried chicken).

You can also get the highly lauded Tugboat—once only available on the weekends—which consists of eggs Benedict on a grilled buttermilk biscuit topped with avocado, two poached eggs, smoked tomato hollandaise, and your choice of ham, fried chicken, maple bacon, house-cured salmon, or heirloom tomatoes. Holy calories, batman!

Type: American
Neighborhood: Eastside
Price: $
Try the: Tugboat, YOLO, Mac on Crack
Great for: Brunch, Pets, Hangovers

Left: Go big and get the Tugboat—eggs Benedict on homemade biscuits with your choice of protein or heirloom tomatoes.

Right: This open-faced breakfast sandwich features house-cured sashimi-grade salmon, a poached egg, and plenty of fried capers.

Anyhow, tasty food aside, I have a few theories on why their demographic skews younger. These mostly have to do with the location, counter service, and seating. But also, hangovers. The Shop serves the perfect eats to cure what ails you. We oldies might like to claim we're too mature to get them, but really we're just not leaving the house after a big night out anymore.

730 North Milpas St.
805-845-1696
yourshopkitchen.com

175

SLY'S

Fresh seafood, prime steaks, and vintage cocktails . . . is your mouth watering yet? Sly's restaurant is a charming fine dining find in Carpinteria, a slightly sleepier beach town about twelve miles south of Santa Barbara.

Chef James Sly's French-inspired menu boasts steaks, oysters, escargots, and of course, steamed mussels served with crisp fries. Having trained as a classical chef in Europe, James refers to himself as a "dinosaur" of traditional, even old-fashioned, cooking. He created Lucky's in Montecito and built it into a premier steakhouse during its first seven years. After leaving Lucky's in 2007, he hatched plans for Sly's and has been busy here ever since.

The entrance to the restaurant feels very European. "Sly's" is spelled out in black and white tile in front of the door, perfect for a shoe shot photo op. The bar area is surrounded by cafe tables and a Vespa is suspended above it. You can eat in here if you like, and at the very least, you should stop for a cocktail before proceeding back to the dining room. The extensive cocktail menu focuses on historic drinks, with the date of origin listed next to each recipe, some going back as far as two hundred years. A delicious happy hour happens from 4 to 6 p.m., including weekends.

Sly's is also a nice place to stop in for a glass or bottle of wine. In fact, Sly's wine list has received the *Wine Spectator* Award of Excellence from 2011 to 2016. From lighthearted whites to rich,

Type: French Steakhouse
Neighborhood: Carpinteria
Price: $$-$$$
Try the: Mussels, Skinny Onion Rings, New York Strip
Great for: Brunch, Happy Hour, Special Occasions

Left: The tilework out front lets you know you're in the right place.

Right: The bar serves a roster of historic cocktails, with some recipes dating back over a century.

complex reds, there's something for everyone. Experience wines from Santa Barbara, Santa Ynez, and France, served at the right temperature and for the right price. What could be better than that? Oh, maybe pairing your wine with a scrumptious sirloin or local abalone, that's what.

One of the most excellent ways to visit Sly's—if you're in Goleta, Santa Barbara, or Ventura, anyway—is by train. Amtrak picks up and lets off across the street from the restaurant. It's a wonderful way to spend a hassle-free day in downtown Carpinteria. You can grab beer or wine from the bar cart on the train, and no one has to drive!

686 Linden Ave., Carpinteria
805-684-6666
slysonline.com

THE SPOT

Order a trusty cheeseburger from the quintessential California burger shack and enjoy a view of the beach while you wait.

Located just past the train tracks on Linden Avenue in downtown Carpinteria, mere steps from the beach, is The Spot: a trusty little restaurant that all the locals know. If you see a small shack with a line at the window, you're in the right place. Serving up delicious hot dogs, fries, and more since 1914, The Spot is Carpinteria's go-to for a quick bite.

The Spot is known for its burgers, chili cheese fries, and onion rings—the kind of hot, fast food that works wonders at refueling surfers who've spent a chilly day in the water. The surprisingly large menu also includes veggie burgers, Mexican specialties like burritos and nachos, and fish and chips. And you should definitely try a milkshake. Each one is made to order with real ice cream, none of this big-batch, premixed nonsense.

There's no dress code, so come in your flip-flops and bikini or trunks, if you please. The Spot is a great place to bring a hungry family. You don't have to worry about noise, service, or picky eaters. There is seating outside, or you can walk across the street to the park for an impromptu picnic. Or take your food and head down the road to the "world's safest beach." Does that mean you don't have to wait half an hour after eating to go swimming? You be the judge!

Type: Fast Food
Neighborhood: Carpinteria
Price: $
Try the: Cheeseburger, Chili Cheese Fries, Shakes
Great for: Kids, Beach Dates, Lunch

Left: This beachfront shack has been serving great food to hungry people since 1914.

Right: Keep it simple with a chili burger and fries with a side of ocean breezes.

After you finish up, there are a lot of other great attractions nearby, including local boutiques, Robitaille's Fine Candies, and Island Brewing Company. Grab a beer, sate your sweet tooth, and check out the heart of downtown Carp. The area can be extremely busy on summer and fall weekends—particularly during the California Avocado Festival, which closes off the street for three days every October—but it's still usually less chaotic than State Street.

One super-important thing to know before you go: The Spot is cash only! No plastic, no Venmo, just good old-fashioned paper dollars. So hit the ATM because this is a can't-miss "beach town" experience when you're in Carpinteria.

398 Linden Ave., Carpinteria
805-684-6311

THE STONEHOUSE

Located at one of the area's poshest and most exclusive hotels, The Stonehouse began life as a nineteenth-century citrus-packing building before being transformed into the luxe dining establishment it is today. It comprises two main areas. There is a lounge area, complete with full bar, and a separate dining room with creekside views and a ceiling that twinkles with lights.

On temperate evenings, you can enjoy your dinner and gaze at the ocean from the peaceful deck. The menu here emphasizes regional cuisine prepared with fruits, vegetables, and herbs harvested from the kitchen's onsite garden. Reservations are recommended.

For an appetizer, you might be tempted by the foie gras, but try the Santa Barbara abalone or hamachi crudo with local uni instead for a true taste of the town. Entrées range from Moroccan spiced chicken tagine to grass-fed steak Diane, flambéed tableside.

Lunch and Sunday brunch are also served. The brunch menu includes delicacies like lobster omelets, prime Wagyu steak, and eggs Benedict with shaved, bone-in prosciutto. The meal is a set price and features your choice of bottomless mimosas, Bellinis, proseccos, or champagne.

Plow & Angel, a more casual eatery, is also located on the property.

San Ysidro Ranch
900 San Ysidro Lane
805-565-1700
sanysidroranch.com/santa-barbara-restaurants

Type: Californian
Neighborhood: Montecito
Price: $$$
Try the: Jumbo Lump Crab Benedict, Classic Steak Diane, Rack of Lamb
Great for: Brunch, Date Night, Celebrations

Top: Located at the elite San Ysidro Ranch, the Stonehouse might be the prettiest restaurant in Santa Barbara.

Above: Dine on the creekside patio for a romantic warm-weather meal.

TAQUERIA EL BAJIO

First, locals call this place El Bajio. Second, you will probably hear it referenced in arguments about the best Mexican food in Santa Barbara. There was even a *Forbes* article about it! Just like there are a lot of La Super-Rica loyalists, there are a lot of ardent El Bajio fans as well. I'm one of them.

It might surprise you to know that El Bajio has been up and running since 1996. For more than two decades, the Guzman family has been serving up delicious tacos and other specialties. Their menu is so vast that it's inaccurate to call them a taqueria, but we'll start there anyway.

The tacos are delicious, slightly larger than your average street tacos. They come with just one homemade tortilla, instead of the more common two, and a range of fillings. The asada and adobada tacos are popular, but the chicharron is an unusual standout. The pork skin is stewed until tender, not crispy, and bathed in a mouthwatering chile verde sauce. El Bajio also has veggie soft tacos as well as crispy bean and potato tacos that even meat eaters crave.

Beyond tacos, there's a lot for a hungry person to choose from here. The burritos are girthy, the gorditas are filling, and the tortas are served on fresh telera rolls with slices of avocado. They have a number of seafood dishes available. The shrimp cocktail is served just like you'll find it in Mexico, with shrimp, onions, and other goodies waiting to be fished out of a large vat of liquidy tomato sauce. And if you like chiles rellenos, you'll definitely enjoy theirs.

My favorite meal at El Bajio is actually breakfast. It's amazing. I'm admittedly addicted to chilaquiles, and theirs have the right

Type: Mexican
Neighborhood: Eastside
Price: $
Try the: Chilaquiles, Pozole, Lengua,
Asada & Chicharron Tacos
Great for: Breakfast, Lunch, Casual Groups

Top left: Taqueria El Bajio has been serving hungry patrons on Milpas for more than 20 years.

Top right: The tacos are a little larger than traditional street tacos and served on homemade tortillas.

Left: Try the crispy Tacos Dorados, which come served in a group of three and have both meat and veggie options.

mix of crunch and give. They have a ton of other huevos dishes as well, including huevos con chorizo, huevos rancheros, and the very traditional huevos a la Mexicana.

Whatever you decide to eat, wash it down with a freshly made horchata or agua fresca. They usually have sandia—watermelon—and it's a refreshing, if sweet, treat that will help you counteract the heat of the salsa bar.

129 North Milpas St.
805-884-1828
elbajiosb.com

TEE-OFF

Hidden in a rather plain-looking strip mall well outside of downtown Santa Barbara, the Tee-Off is the kind of place you might drive past for years without going inside. And that would be a real shame.

The Tee-Off opened in 1964, and it's a gem of a steakhouse that feels like a treasure from a bygone era. The first hint that it might be something special comes from the neon signs promising "Prime Ribs," "Cocktails," and "Tee-Off Fried Chicken" that line its windowless exterior. As soon as you step through the heavy door into the dimly lit and deliciously scented interior, you'll know you're in the right place. At least if you're hungry.

The bar inside is a comfortable spot to have a drink. It has friendly bartenders, sports on TV, and a padded rail for resting your weary elbows. Tony holds court here, and he makes a mean manhattan. Other classic cocktails are just as easy to come by. If you're dining alone or with just a few people, eating at the bar is a fun experience.

As the name suggests, the Tee-Off carries a golf theme throughout the restaurant, most notably on the menu. There you'll find its signature dish—prime rib—served in a variety of sizes, from the Par Cut (ten ounces) to the Double Eagle (double bone-in).

Every meal begins with a classic vegetable tray. Dinner entrées from the main menu come with soup and salad as well as your choice of rice or potato, a side vegetable, and sourdough rolls. For soup, you can choose from either clam chowder or prime rib, so it's not exactly a light meal. In a land of kale smoothies and poke bowls, this is a feast that really sticks to your ribs.

Type: Steakhouse
Neighborhood: Upper State
Price: $$-$$$
Try the: Manhattan, Clam Chowder, Prime Rib
Great for: Dates, Celebrations, Bar Dining

Left: A traditional-style steakhouse, The Tee-Off is immediately recognizable by the neon out front.

Right: Sink into a comfortable booth or saddle up to the bar.

The back page offers the Club Menu, a selection of ever-so-slightly lighter dishes like fish and chips (no soup and salad) and the Tee-Off Burger, which definitely has its own local fan club.

This restaurant is wonderfully dark and cozy, but it's never quiet. It's still a lively destination, even on weeknights, more than fifty years after it first opened its doors in the same location.

Like the sign out front says, it is "Air Conditioned." That and the lack of windows make the Tee-Off a great place to duck into for a cool drink from Tony on a hot summer day. Just make sure you're not seated anywhere near the kitchen because that part of the house is always on fire . . . in a good, but also hot, way.

3627 State St.
805-687-1616
teeoffsb.com

THREE PICKLES

Don't go to Three Pickles if you prefer dainty sandwiches. They don't serve that kind here. What they do dish up is a bunch of big, messy, melty deli creations built to satisfy hungry appetites. Oh, and they have salads too.

Three Pickles started out in a smaller location next door, but the line was so long they soon had to expand into the space at the historic Jimmy's Oriental Gardens property.

They make some great sandwiches here. There are deli stacks, kind of your classic cold-cut sammies served on rye, sourdough, or Italian roll. Then they have their hot melty specialties. Try the Presidio Pastrami or the Canon Capicolla Club for a lunch that will leave you more than full.

Perhaps most unique to this place is the roster of "Subs Our Way." These rolls are filled with your choice of meats and cheeses, then piled high with diced tomatoes, onions, and dill pickles, dressed with oil, and sprinkled with oregano.

There is a pickle and pepperoncini bar, and cold beer is served on draft. Three Pickles also owns The Pickle Room next door, a great bar open in the evenings.

Three Pickles has a location in Goleta too, which is good news for a lot of students and workers who are based in the area, not to mention local Goletians!

126 East Canon Perdido St.
805-965-1015
threepickles.com

Type: Deli
Neighborhood: Downtown
Price: $
Try the: Subs Our Way, Presidio Pastrami, Clam Chowder (Fridays only)
Great for: Lunch, Single Diners, Take Out

Getting a sub made "our way" at Three Pickles means it comes loaded with diced tomatoes, onions, and pickles and is sprinkled with oregano.

TINO'S ITALIAN GROCERY

Depending on which door you use, this place looks just like a grocery store when you first enter. There are aisles of bottles, cans, bags, and boxes—most containing wonderful things—but don't get distracted.

You have a mission. And that mission is to get up to the deli counter quickly, before the line gets any longer.

When you finally get to the counter, don't blow it. Are you ready? It's time to order a sandwich. Yep, that's what you're here for! One of the tastiest sandwiches in town is waiting to meet you at this charming Italian grocery shop.

It's pretty simple because there really aren't that many options. (But don't worry, the very cool Tino's team won't bat an eyelash if you start getting a little complicated.) You can order the Regular, Deluxe, or Super Deluxe.

The Regular is a combination of Molinari salami, capocollo, galantina, two way, and Swiss and American cheese on an Italian roll spread with mayo, mustard, and oil. The Deluxe steps it up a notch, adding tomato and shredded lettuce.

But the Super Deluxe, that's the one you want. It has all the toppings of the other two, plus pepperoncini and ham. Unless you're just a meat and cheese kind of a person. Then maybe stick with the Regular. It's seriously great too.

And sure, you can get a little fancy with your sandwich order. You can add a meat here, subtract one there. You can go full vegetarian even, in which case they chop up some giardiniera and stick it in there with the cheese.

When your sandwich is just how you like it, they roll it up in some deli paper, tape it off, and pack it in a bag with a stack of napkins. You

Type: Deli
Neighborhood: Downtown
Price: $
Try the: Super Deluxe
Great for: Lunch, Picnics, Take Out

Top left: The original Tino's was opened in 1947. This location opened in 2014.

Above left: Shop for Italian specialty foods while you wait for your order.

Above right: Tino's signature sandwich is the Super Deluxe, a fully loaded sub stacked with Molinari salami, capocollo, galantina, ham, shredded lettuce, tomatoes, pepperoncini, red onions, and Swiss and American cheese on an Italian roll spread with mayo, mustard, and oil.

can take it to go—it travels well—or eat it at one of the small tables in the shop.

Although Tino's as it exists now opened in 2015 there's a long local history that goes along with this deli. The original Tino took over the Italian Grocery and Bakery in 1947. Although he eventually sold the bakery part, he and his family ran the grocery and sold sandwiches until he passed in 2014.

Not long after that location closed, this one was opened by the next generation under the guidance of Tino's sister, Terry, who had worked with him closely for many decades.

Although the building is new, the sandwiches are still pretty much the same salty, oily wonders that they always were. To miss a stop here would be to miss out on a piece of Santa Barbara history.

210 West Carrillo St.
805-966-6041
tinositaliangrocery.com

TWENTY-FOUR BLACKBIRDS

Chocolatier Mike Orlando is a scientist, and I'm pretty sure that's why his chocolate is so good. Over at Twenty-Four Blackbirds, he's crafting up handmade artisan chocolate bars and truffles that would make Willy Wonka weep with joy.

"I taught myself to make chocolate while I was working as an analytical chemist at UCSB. The more I learned about chocolate manufacturing, the more interested I became," said Orlando.

What started in his kitchen with a pound of cocoa beans is now a small-scale artisan chocolate company, serving over four hundred retail customers nationwide. He uses high-quality cocoa beans that are hand selected and sorted from estates and plantations all over the world to create single-origin delights on specialty equipment he builds himself.

Twenty-Four Blackbirds's prices are extremely reasonable, so you won't feel guilty if you go a little overboard. You can order single bars, sampler packs, and drinking chocolates online and have them shipped. It's the perfect Santa Barbara sweet treat to send as a gift.

Type: Chocolate
Price: $
Try the: Single-Origin Dark Chocolate Bars,
Vanilla Salted Caramels

Left: Bags of cacao beans straight from the source.

Center: How chocolate marshmallows get their start.

Right: Orlando's best known product: affordable single-origin chocolate bars made right here in Santa Barbara.

You'll also find Orlando's chocolate at businesses all over town. Sama Sama uses them in desserts, and Handlebar Coffee Roasters includes them in hot chocolates and mochas. Looking for something a little more adult? "Figueroa Mountain and Third Window Brewing both offer beers using my cocoa nibs," he added during our chat. That sounds great to me!

twentyfourblackbirds.com

TYDES RESTAURANT

Here's the problem with including this place in the book: there's a pretty big chance you can't go. It is literally off limits to most people. But that also makes it super unique, right?

Here's the other thing that makes it undeniably distinctive. The bar is a coral reef. Before or after your meal, you absolutely must stop for a drink at the Coral Reef Bar, a partially outdoor twenty-eight-foot oval seawater aquarium bar full of fish, shrimp, and live coral. If you can get in, that is.

The Coral Casino Beach and Cabana Club is not a casino but a private beach club, perched above Butterfly Beach just across from the Four Seasons Resort The Biltmore Santa Barbara. In the fall of 1936, the Biltmore Hotel's owner, Robert Odell, launched plans for a grand social club where prominent families of the area and Hollywood's elite could gather. Since its grand opening in 1937, the Coral Casino has hosted some of the world's foremost dignitaries, Hollywood stars, musicians, and philanthropists.

Today, after a careful rehabilitation from 2005 to 2008, the Coral Casino is as stunningly exclusive as ever. It's home to an oceanfront larger-than-Olympic-sized swimming pool, private cabanas, a fitness center, and three onsite eateries.

The Tydes is the most delicious of them all. Open only to Coral Casino club members and overnight guests of the resort, the restaurant features Mediterranean flavors and seasonal ingredients with an emphasis on seafood. Marco Fossati, a transplanted Italian from Genoa, is the executive chef here at the Tydes as well as the Bella Vista at the resort.

Type: Mediterranean
Neighborhood: Montecito
Price: $$-$$$
Try the: Oysters, Wagyu Tenderloin, King Salmon
Great for: Cocktails, Ocean Views, Fancy Dinners

Top right: The most striking attraction at Tydes is the live coral reef bar.

Above left: Visit with sea creatures while sipping cocktails and enjoying the ocean view.

Above right: Tydes is on the top floor of the Coral Casino, directly facing Butterfly Beach.

His lunch and dinner menus are simple and elegant, complementing both the architecture of the Coral Casino and the ocean views. Lunch is divided into cold and hot dishes, ranging from hamachi sashimi and artichoke salad to miso black cod and seared scallops. For dinner, you might start with caviar and cauliflower, move on to charred octopus, and then tuck into a whole branzino or squid-ink pasta carbonara topped with Santa Barbara uni.

While it is very relaxing to eat in the Tydes's posh dining room, I think it's fun to grab a bite at the bar too. Where else can you sip a specialty cocktail in the sunshine while anemones bloom and sway underneath your glass? A simple bar bites menu offers fresh oysters, crudités, and flatbread—plenty to fill your belly.

The real trick, of course, is getting inside, unless you're a guest at the Four Seasons Resort The Biltmore Santa Barbara—then you're a shoo-in!

Coral Casino Beach and Cabana Club
1281 Channel Dr.
805-969-2261
coralcasinoclub.com

VIA MAESTRA 42

Tucked away on landlocked upper State Street is a romantic jewel of an Italian eatery, Via Maestra 42. The restaurant is very small and, at first glance, barely resembles a restaurant at all. There are cases full of Italian delicacies, displays of tasty takeaway items, and a few small tables set with fresh roses inside. There are also a couple of cafe tables jostling for space outside on the narrow sidewalk.

Do not let this small-town appearance negatively affect your decision to eat here. It is one of the best dining experiences you will have in town, from the menu and wine list to the service and atmosphere. Every dish is delicious and authentic. Don't be surprised if you feel like you have been transported to Italy. The waiters' accents—real or not, I'm never quite sure—add to the charm.

Via Maestra 42 opened in 2000 in order to showcase the Italian products owner Renato Moiso had been supplying to restaurants in the area since 1993. Named after the street where Renato was born, the restaurant is full of memories. Postcards and notes frame the entryway, including one from Julia Child herself.

The food is consistently heavenly. The pasta is neither over- nor underdone, the sauces are unique, and special meat dishes are exactly that, special. The wine menu may seem intimidatingly long, but there are some true gems on there. The servers are well trained in helping you select bottles and glasses according to your preference, so there's no need to hesitate.

You can get smaller portions of many of the same pasta dishes at lunch for a reasonable price. Lunch is less formal. You order from the counter and then sit while your meal is prepared and brought to your

Type: Italian
Neighborhood: Upper State
Price: $$-$$$
Try the: Linguine al Vongole, Ravioli Zuccotto, Dark Chocolate Gelato
Great for: Breakfast, Dates, Special Occasions

Top left: This Italian restaurant is tucked among shops on upper State Street.

Left center: Breakfast at Via Maestra 42 is one of Santa Barbara's best-kept secrets.

Above left: Whether you're dining in or not, you should stop by for a scoop of gelato.

Above right: Inside, it's warm, cozy, and always lively for dinner.

table. If you're in a hurry, you can get one of the sandwiches from the case, usually some combination of meats, cheeses, and roasted vegetables piled high on a piece of fresh focaccia.

Or you can go for broke and skip straight to gelato. Via Maestra 42 has a nice selection of gelatos and sorbets you can eat in or take to go. Probably the best way to eat it is mounded into the center of one of their apricot croissants. That's right, you can get really gourmet ice cream sandwiches here.

Breakfast at Via Maestra 42 is one of Santa Barbara's best-kept secrets. Prices are affordable, and flavors are bright. Perhaps unsurprisingly, they make a nice cappuccino here. Plates of eggs served with prosciutto and eggplant are often accompanied by slices of fresh melon and followed by chunks of sugared ricotta. It's an incredibly satisfying way to start your day. Just keep in mind that they don't serve breakfast on Sunday.

3343 State St.
805-569-6522
viamaestra42.com

WILDWOOD KITCHEN

If you fancy a taste of barbecue while you're in Santa Barbara, Wildwood Kitchen is the place to go. Get California smokehouse flavors in an upscale setting (read: with real silverware and cocktails) when you visit this restaurant in a newly hip area on the edge of downtown.

"My dad owned a barbecue restaurant when I was growing up," said Justin West, owner and chef, about the origins of Wildwood Kitchen. "He passed away six years ago, so in a way opening this place brought his legacy back to life. And Santa Barbara was in desperate need of a real barbecue joint!"

He's not wrong about that. Although the Central Coast is known for Santa Maria-style tri-tip—a cut of beef that is rubbed with spices and then grilled over indirect heat—real slow-smoked barbecue has been significantly harder to come by. Until now.

You'll find brisket, ribs, chicken, and more at Wildwood, with all the classic sides, like beans, potato salad, and cole slaw. And this isn't cheater barbecue! West and his crew use a Southern Pride smoker to slow-smoke the fresh, never-frozen meats over a period of hours. Wildwood's butcher, Richard Lewis, makes all the sausages in house in addition to grinding beef for burgers and curing and smoking bacon.

Whether you're stumped for what to try or just really hungry, Westin has some advice for you. "Our best-selling item is our sampler plate. We offer two sizes. The BBQ Sampler has all the smoked meats. The BBQ King Sampler has all the meats *and* all the sausages. Add a few side dishes and it's a party!"

Type: BBQ
Neighborhood: Downtown/Eastside
Price: $$
Try the: Pulled Pork Sandwich, Mac & Cheese, Frito Pie
Great for: Lunch, Patio Cocktails, Meat Lovers

Top left: Check out the Triple Chop, a combination of BBQ meats, pickles, and sliced onions on a brioche bun.

Above left: The side dishes are hearty too. Shown: the root vegetable salad (seasonal) with fries.

Above right: If you see this sign, you're in the right place.

Unlike more traditional southern barbecue shops, Wildwood also has California-approved healthy options. For example, there are salads made with kale and little gem greens sourced from local farmers. You can even get them topped with meat for a small extra charge. Because the Wildwood team shops at the local farmers' market on Tuesdays and Saturdays, many of their vegetable dishes change with the season.

It's no fluke that Wildwood has been drawing a crowd since it opened. (A friend of mine recently spotted Conan O'Brien dining there.) West has been cooking in Santa Barbara for a long time, having opened and helmed popular restaurant Julienne for more than eight years. "I like the Santa Barbara food scene because of the raw ingredients we have at our disposal. We're really fortunate."

410 East Haley St.
805-845-3995
wildwoodkitchensb.com

YELLOW BELLY

Yellow Belly is a welcoming beer bar and restaurant just off the beaten path in Santa Barbara. Tucked in a mainly residential neighborhood, it's a real locals' place—exactly what you hope to discover when you're visiting.

At first approach, it looks kind of like a little house. There's a wide deck at the front and comfortable furniture in the entryway. You can choose from indoor, outdoor, and bar seating. There's also an intimate back deck with just a few tall tables.

When it was first opened by two friends in 2014, Yellow Belly was billed as a beer bar with food. Besties Alex Noormand and Tracy Clark succeeded in their goal of creating a place to kick back and relax while enjoying a brew. It has ten craft beer taps that are in constant rotation. You can call ahead to see what's pouring or just head in and take your chances.

More importantly, there's food! In addition to draft beer and Central Coast wines, Yellow Belly has a menu that has expanded rapidly in response to the overwhelming support they received from the surrounding community. It's the spot to go for brunch or dinner in the Oak Park area. Dishes are tasty, the prices are fair, and the atmosphere is always inviting.

Dinner items include comfort classics like homemade pizza, burgers, and mac 'n' cheese, with some crisp salads and fresh vegetables mixed in. The warm pretzel with cheese dipping sauce pairs perfectly with cold suds, and the fried chicken sandwich with jalapeño slaw is a local favorite. You can put an egg on just about anything here, but it's probably best perched atop caramelized

Type: American
Neighborhood: Oak Park
Price: $$
Try the: Fried Chicken Sandwich, Brussels Sprouts, Cornbread Benedict
Great for: Friends, Families, Everyone

Top left: Opened by two best friends, Yellow Belly is a beer bar with great food.

Top right: The buttermilk fried chicken with pickled onion and cabbage and jalapeño slaw is a best seller. Photo by Silas Fallstich

Above left: It's hard to go wrong with a burger and a beer. Try stepping it up by adding an egg. Photo by Silas Fallstich

Above right: Yellow Belly is open for brunch on the weekends. Photo by Silas Fallstich

Brussels sprouts or tucked into the middle of a melty grilled cheese.

Yellow Belly dishes up brunch on the weekends only. Swing by for bottomless mimosas, bananas foster waffles, and cornbread eggs Benedict.

The restaurant sources from many Santa Barbara-based providers. It serves Handlebar coffee and McConnell's ice cream, and it always has a locally brewed beer or two in the lineup.

Reservations are not accepted, but gluten-free and vegan diners are. Live bands usually play on Saturday nights. And pet dogs are welcome on the patio.

2611 De La Vina St.
805-770-5694
yellowbellytap.com

YOICHI'S

There might not be a more impressive meal in Santa Barbara than the dinner you will have at Yoichi's. Sure, you can find friendly service in a lot of places, and you may even find food that suits your own particular palate better. But for a combination of food, service, and meditative atmosphere, you can't top the only kaiseki restaurant in town.

If you're an old kaiseki pro, go ahead and skip down a paragraph or two. If you're not, though, you're probably wondering what it is. Kaiseki is a traditional multicourse Japanese meal that's sometimes compared to French haute cuisine in terms of sophistication, preparation, and care.

A kaiseki dinner menu varies according to the seasons and what's available locally. It is said that it's a meal at one with nature, so it's not uncommon to find natural elements like flowers and leaves plated with your dishes. Dishes are made fresh and brought in succession, with food and tableware complementing and contrasting in color, shape, and texture.

At Yoichi's, you'll want to make reservations ahead of time to enjoy their traditional seven-course meal. You'll be served assorted appetizers, soup, sashimi, a grilled dish, a steamed or simmered dish, sushi, and dessert. Some courses will present you with options, and others, like the sashimi, come as a surprise based on what was fresh at the market that day.

Sample dishes include lobster with red miso, oysters in a steamed citrus bowl, and local abalone—but don't set your heart on anything, because the menu is always changing. The meal is expertly served at

Type: Japanese
Neighborhood: Downtown
Price: $$$
Try the: Set Menu
Great for: Adventurous Eaters, Impressing a Date

Left: Yoichi's is a one-of-a-kind find serving authentic kaiseki cuisine.

Center: Every item is crafted with care, from the thoughtful presentation to the handmade ceramic dishes.

Right: The sashimi course varies based on what is fresh at the fish market. Shown here served with a fin from one of the day's selections. Photo by Aron Ives

a leisurely pace. Allow yourself two hours or so from start to finish. Your server will be able to answer all your questions about where certain items come from and how they are made.

Yoichi's also has a handsome sake selection that has been carefully curated to pair with the menu. There's a chance you won't recognize any of them from your experiences at local sushi shops, so ask the knowledgeable staff for guidance.

Both the food and the beverages are presented in striking ceramic wear. Each dish is different, handmade by a Japanese artisan who lives locally. If you are dining with a group, you'll want to take a moment to admire your companions' cups, bowls, and plates.

A smaller four-course menu is sometimes available at Yoichi's too; call ahead to be sure. But unless you're one of the lucky ones who frequently tucks into a kaiseki meal, you should really treat yourself to the seven-course option. It's a dining experience you won't soon forget.

230 East Victoria St.
805-962-6627
yoichis.com

RESTAURANTS A-Z

The Andersen's Danish
Bakery & Restaurant
1106 State St.
Santa Barbara

Arigato Sushi
1225 State St.
Santa Barbara

Arnoldi's Cafe
600 Olive St.
Santa Barbara

Backyard Bowls
331 Motor Way
Santa Barbara

Bella Vista
1260 Channel Dr.
Santa Barbara

The Black Sheep
26 East Ortega St.
Santa Barbara

The Blue Owl
5 West Canon Perdido St.
Santa Barbara

Boathouse
2981 Cliff Dr.
Santa Barbara

Bouchon
9 West Victoria St.
Santa Barbara

The Brewhouse
229 West Montecito St.
Santa Barbara

Brophy Bros.
119 Harbor Way
Santa Barbara

C'est Cheese
825 Santa Barbara St.
Santa Barbara

Ca'Dario
37 East Victoria St.
Santa Barbara

Cajun Kitchen
901 Chapala St.
Santa Barbara

Chase Bar & Grill
1012 State St.
Santa Barbara

China Pavilion
1202 Chapala St.
Santa Barbara

Chuck's of Hawaii
3888 State St.
Santa Barbara

Cold Spring Tavern
5995 Stagecoach Rd.
Santa Barbara

Corazón Cocina
38 West Victoria St.
Santa Barbara

D'Angelo Bread
25 West Gutierrez St.
Santa Barbara

Dave's Dogs
134 South Milpas St.
Santa Barbara

Downey's
1305 State St.
Santa Barbara

Dutch Garden
4203 State St.
Santa Barbara

East Beach Tacos
226 South Milpas St.
Santa Barbara

Empty Bowl Gourmet
Noodle Bar
38 West Victoria St. #109
Santa Barbara

Farmer Boy Restaurant
3427 State St.
Santa Barbara

Flavor of India
3026 State St.
Santa Barbara

The French Press
528 Anacapa St.
Santa Barbara

Garrett's Old Fashioned
Restaurant
2001 State St.
Santa Barbara

The Habit Burger Grill
5735 Hollister Ave.
Goleta

Harry's Plaza Cafe
3313 State St.
Santa Barbara

The Hitching Post II
406 East Highway 246
Buellton

Il Fustino
3401 State St.
Santa Barbara

Industrial Eats
181 Industrial Way
Buellton

Intermezzo
819 Anacapa St.
Santa Barbara

Jane
1311 State St.
Santa Barbara

Kanaloa Seafood
715 Chapala St.
Santa Barbara

La Chapala Market
5780 Hollister Ave.
Goleta

La Super-Rica Taqueria
622 North Milpas St.
Santa Barbara

The Lark
131 Anacapa St.
Santa Barbara

Lilac Patisserie
1017 State St.
Santa Barbara

Lilly's Taqueria
310 Chapala St.
Santa Barbara

Lito's Mexican Restaurant
514 East Haley St.
Santa Barbara

Loquita
202 State St.
Santa Barbara

Los Agaves
600 North Milpas St.
Santa Barbara

2911 De La Vina St.
Santa Barbara

7024 Market Place Dr.
Goleta

Lucky Penny
127 Anacapa St.
Santa Barbara

Lucky's
1279 Coast Village Rd.
Santa Barbara

McConnell's Fine Ice Creams
728 State St.
Santa Barbara

Mesa Verde
1919 Cliff Dr.
Santa Barbara

Metropulos
216 East Yanonali St.
Santa Barbara

Mony's Mexican Food
217 Anacapa St.
Santa Barbara

The Natural Cafe
6990 Marketplace Dr.
Goleta

The Natural Cafe
508 State St.
361 Hitchcock Way
Santa Barbara

Noodle City
5869 Hollister Ave.
Goleta

Nook
116 Santa Barbara St.
Santa Barbara

Norton's Pastrami and Deli
18 West Figueroa St.
Santa Barbara

Olio Cucina
11 West Victoria St.
Santa Barbara

On The Alley
117 Harbor Way
Santa Barbara

Outpost
5650 Calle Real
Goleta

Padaro Beach Grill
3766 Santa Claus Lane
Carpinteria

The Palace Grill
8 East Cota St.
Santa Barbara

The Palms
701 Linden Ave.
Carpinteria

Paradise Cafe
702 Anacapa St.
Santa Barbara

The Pickle Room
126 East Canon Perdido St.
Santa Barbara

Presidio Market
1236 Santa Barbara St.
Santa Barbara

Renaud's Patisserie & Bistro
3315 State St.
Santa Barbara

Rose Café
1816 Cliff Dr.
Santa Barbara

Rusty's Pizza
5250 Carpinteria
Carpinteria

Rusty's Pizza
270 Storke Rd.
5934 Calle Real
Goleta

Rusty's Pizza
414 North Milpas St.
3731 State St.
232 West Carrillo St.
149 South Turnpike Rd.
111 State St.
Santa Barbara

Sama Sama Kitchen
1208 State St.
Santa Barbara

Santa Barbara Shellfish
Company
230 Stearns Wharf
Santa Barbara

Scarlett Begonia
11 West Victoria St. #10
Santa Barbara

Shintori Sushi Factory
3001 State St.
Santa Barbara

The Shop American Kitchen
730 North Milpas St.
Santa Barbara

Sly's
686 Linden Ave.
Carpinteria

The Spot
398 Linden Ave.
Carpinteria

The Stonehouse
900 San Ysidro Lane
Santa Barbara

Taqueria El Bajio
129 North Milpas St.
Santa Barbara

Tee-Off
3627 State St.
Santa Barbara

Three Pickles
126 East Canon Perdido St.
Santa Barbara

Tino's Italian Grocery
210 West Carrillo St.
Santa Barbara

Tydes Restaurant
1281 Channel Dr.
Santa Barbara

Via Maestra 42
3343 State St.
Santa Barbara

Wildwood Kitchen
410 East Haley St.
Santa Barbara

Yellow Belly
2611 De La Vina St.
Santa Barbara

Yoichi's
230 East Victoria St.
Santa Barbara

RESTAURANTS BY TYPE

CALIFORNIAN FRENCH
Bouchon, 18
Downey's, 44

CAFE
Andersen's Danish Bakery & Restaurant, The, 2
C'est Cheese, 26
Lilac Patisserie, 84

CAJUN
Cajun Kitchen, 28
Palace Grill, The, 142

CHOCOLATE
Jessica Foster Confections, 74
Twenty-Four Blackbirds, 190

CHINESE
China Pavilion, 32
Pickle Room, The, 148

COFFEEHOUSE
French Press, The, 56

DELI
Metropulos, 120
Norton's Pastrami and Deli, 130
Three Pickles, 186
Tino's Italian Grocery, 188

DESSERT
McConnell's Fine Ice Creams, 116

DINER
Farmer Boy Restaurant, 52
Garrett's Old Fashioned Restaurant, 58

FAST FOOD
Spot, The, 178

FRENCH STEAKHOUSE
Sly's, 176

GERMAN
Dutch Garden, 46

APPENDIX

WEST BEACH

.COM